THE YOUNG CHARLES LAMB

The Young Charles Lamb

TRUDY WEST

Illustrated by
Susan E. Sims

ROY PUBLISHERS, INC. – NEW YORK

LIBRARY OF CONGRESS
CATALOG CARD NO. 65-18881

PRINTED IN GREAT BRITAIN

CONTENTS

I

The Boy in the Temple

The little boy stood on tiptoe eagerly watching the old sundial in the quiet square within the Temple.

Perhaps if he waited long enough he would see that dark line move on. He held his breath, waiting for the miracle which he always hoped for and which never happened. His dreamy eyes grew serious and puzzled as he pushed back the lock of black hair impeding his view. The line *must* move some time because it was never in the same place twice when he looked at it! Why, then, couldn't he see it?

He was so absorbed in this fascinating mystery that he did not notice the approach of two of the Benchers of the Inner Temple as they paced the terrace on their usual morning walk.

Mr Thomas Coventry walked as if he were marching at the head of a column, his huge form overshadowing his slighter companion. His tread was elephantine, his face was square and ferocious and he growled like a lion when he spoke, or so the children of the Temple thought.

The two eminent lawyers paused in their walk.

'Who's that boy over there?' Mr Coventry asked Mr Salt.

'That's the youngest of the Lamb children – Charles,' Samuel Salt answered mildly.

'Lamb? He's our second waiter, isn't he?'

'Yes, and my scrivener as well. His wife keeps my chambers. A good couple, but it's to be hoped young Charles is the last of their family. Seven's too many in their position – it's almost a blessing they lost four of 'em. A little weakness, you know.' Mr Salt tapped his head significantly.

'H'm. This brat looks intelligent enough.' Mr Coventry dived his hand under the big flap on the pocket of his old-fashioned red waistcoat and brought out a palmful of snuff which he inhaled vigorously as he resumed his stately pacing.

At the sound of the heavy tread the boy at the sundial turned, his thin, wiry frame poised for flight.

'Boy! Come here! I want to talk to you!' Thomas Coventry roared. Clouds of snuff broke from each nostril, darkening the air around him.

Charles thought he looked like a great fiery dragon and ran off in terror.

Number Two Crown Office Row was one of a stately line of buildings facing the garden and the river, and as the boy reached up to the familiar door knob he felt he had reached sanctuary. This was his home, the place where he was born four years ago – on 10th February, 1775, to be exact – and he loved every corner of these quiet cloisters.

The door to the Lambs' set of rooms was on the latch and the small boy ran in. He knew his mother would be at work in Mr Salt's chambers, but Aunt Hetty would be there – she was always there. She might be at what she called her 'devotions' in her room.

He found her in the kitchen, busily splitting French beans and dropping them into a china basin of water, muttering to herself as she did so. The fresh smell of the vegetables was soothing and homely and Charles went to his aunt silently and put his arms about her neck.

Her stern old face relaxed in a smile at the sight of her favourite nephew.

'Why, Charley, what's the matter?'

'N-nothing,' stammered the boy, 'I – I just wanted to see *you*.'

Aunt Hetty put the bowl of beans aside and took the child on her lap.

'Well, I won't deny I'm busy, but I've always got time to spare for the only person in the world I love!'

'That's me!' said Charles confidently, snuggling a little closer. His fear of Thomas Coventry began to fade.

'Yes, that's you!' his aunt gave him a little hug. Her brother, John, was well blessed with this child, she reflected.

'Why don't you love anybody else?' the boy asked curiously.

'It's hard to love people who see nothing but faults in you.' The old lady's face set stubbornly.

'That's Mama, isn't it? I heard you say she was always trying to teach you to be polite.'

'Then you're a naughty boy to listen to what grown-ups say.'

'But it's true, isn't it? You and Mama don't love each other. I know it.'

'You know too much!' Aunt Hetty spoke sharply and Charles slid off her knee. 'Some folks have no respect for others, that's all. Though I'd like to know how they'd do without the bit of money they bring in!' she added darkly. 'Now, get along with you, do. I've got my work to finish. Go and find some nice books to look at.'

'All right.' The boy stood there, waiting for a kiss of dismissal, but the odd look his aunt gave him from under her spectacles scared him away, like it did when he caught her muttering her prayers aloud.

He went into the sitting-room to get some of his favourite books. His father had a good collection, but not half so good as those in Mr Salt's library where Mary took him sometimes.

Charles dragged a chair to the bookshelves and climbed up to reach some of his treasures. He could see Stackhouse's *History of the Bible* up there, on a high shelf, and by standing on tiptoe he could just manage to drag the heavy volumes out of their place.

He felt very proud of his feat as he took the books on to the hearth rug where, lying flat on his stomach, he began to look at the pictures. He turned the pages to find some of the Bible stories he had heard read in Church, but was puzzled when he saw them set out with something called an 'objection' underneath each one, followed by the 'solution'.

The four year old boy barely understood what he read and felt lost in a maze of puzzled doubts.

He paused at the picture of the Witch of Endor, then hastily turned over the page. He did not like it. That terrible old witch! Suppose he met her in the night?

Anxious to forget her he turned back until he came to the much loved story of Noah and the Ark.

His sister Mary came into the room and smiled at the familiar sight of her little brother sprawled upon the rug with a book. She looked over his shoulder and saw the picture of the animals.

'Why, Charley, you'll wear that book out!' she laughed.

He looked up at her with the sweet, gentle smile that was so like her own. At fourteen she was almost grown up, yet not too grown up to share a child's delights.

'Mary, what would happen to us if there should be another Flood?'

'There won't be another one. God promised that.'

'But *if* there should be – ' the boy persisted, 'we'd have to build another Ark, wouldn't we? I wonder how many rooms there would be to hold all the world?'

'It wouldn't hold all the world. It would leave the wicked people out, like it did before.'

Charles pondered this gravely and examined the picture again.

'There's lots of rooms in this one and they're all full of animals.' A grubby forefinger traced the various creatures whose heads were seen protruding from windows. Others were pictured walking up a kind of ramp, in pairs.

'Look, Mary! There are two giraffes! Won't their

heads stick out and get wet? Oh, look, what's this? An elephant – ' he stumbled over the word – 'and a camel, in the front rooms!'

In his excitement he turned over the page too quickly. There was a nasty tearing sound as his two fingers went straight through the unfortunate elephant and camel, leaving gaping holes in the paper.

'Oh, Charley, look what you've done now!' Mary was horrified.

The boy scrambled to his feet and tears sprang to his eyes.

'I – I c-couldn't help it! It just *w-went*!'

There was no time to cover up the misdeed before Mrs Lamb came into the room, hot and tired from preparing Mr Salt's dinner. It seemed to her small son that she looked taller and more stately than ever as she stood looking down at the damaged book, her lips drawn tightly together in anger.

'Give me the book!' she said coldly.

Without a word Mary picked up the two volumes of Stackhouse and handed them to her mother.

'I'll have to keep them under lock and key if you can't be trusted not to destroy them.'

'I'm s-sorry, Mama!' Charles stammered tearfully, 'p-please don't take them away!'

Mrs Lamb took no notice but turned to Mary.

'I can't trust you to look after your brother for five minutes, it seems! But there, I suppose you've got too much of your father's family in you to accept responsibility!' She swept out of the room, clutching the books to her as Charles fought to keep back the tears.

Mary sat down, oppressed by a sense of injustice. There was a brooding look in her dark eyes.

'I wonder why I can never do anything to please my mother?'

Aunt Hetty stood in the doorway of the kitchen, a bitter, twisted smile on her face, as if she knew the secret of this divided household.

Charles, blinded with tears, ran out of the room and went straight to his favourite place on the river bank. He flung himself down on the grass and watched the gently flowing water, waiting for the hurt to heal. Why, oh why, didn't grown-ups *understand*?

Some time later John came looking for him.

'Come along, Charley, no sulks! Dinner's ready!'

Charles turned a tear-stained face to his brother.

'I-I'm not sulking!'

'Well, whatever happened, forget it anyway. Look — I'll give you a pick-a-back if you like, like I used to when you were ill.'

The little boy's face brightened and he looked up at his big, handsome brother with hero-worship in his eyes.

'Hurry up,' said John, not unkindly, 'I've got to go into the City this afternoon.'

Charles clambered on to the broad back.

'May I come too, John?'

'No, of course not. I'm going on *business* — '

'What's business?'

'You wouldn't understand,' the lordly fifteen-year-old scoffed as he began to jog-trot back to the house, 'I'm going to be a clerk soon.'

Charles started to say, 'What's a clerk?' but stopped in time. John might get angry and put him down and he was so enjoying this ride. His brother seldom had time for play these days — he was much too grown up.

'Faster, John!' he urged, 'faster!'

John obligingly galloped right into the sitting-room and dumped young Charles on to the nearest chair. They were both laughing and breathless, and Mrs Lamb paused, with a dish of steaming vegetables in her hands, to look anxiously at John. He was the apple of her eye.

'You shouldn't be tiring yourself like that, Johnnie. Charley's getting big now.'

'Big?' John laughed as he good-naturedly tweaked his young brother's ear. 'Why, there's nothing of him! He needs to eat more big dinners!'

The family settled down to a substantial midday meal. Nobody waited for John Lamb senior who was busy waiting on the barristers in the Temple dining hall. He put in odd appearances now and again and it was not until the table was cleared that he managed to get in for a 'breather' as he put it.

Charles was alone in the room and watched his father warily as he threw himself into an armchair. The boy dragged a footstool along the floor and settled it under his father's feet.

'A-ah, that's better!' the tired man gave a sigh of contentment. 'You're a thoughtful boy, Charley.' He took a closer look at his small son's worried face. 'Why, what's the matter? Been up to mischief?'

Charles blurted out the story of the torn book and ended by saying tearfully, 'I-I'm sorry, Papa!'

Mr Lamb laughed indulgently.

'Of course you are – knowing you and your passion for books! Never mind, boy, don't worry about it. What's done can't be undone.'

Charles smiled again. Papa was never angry; he nearly always laughed things away.

'What about a little read, eh?' Mr Lamb reached out for

the manuscript book on the shelf beside him. He turned the pages slowly, looking with satisfaction at each one filled with his own neat script. He paused.

'Look! I wrote this little thing yesterday. Like to hear it?'

'Oh, yes, please!' Charles loved to hear his father's rhymes. They were so full of fun and happiness.

John Lamb read well, putting the utmost expression into the lines, here a laugh, there a sigh, and the boy listened intently, his intelligent face registering every change of emotion.

'There, my boy,' his father said with pride when he had finished, 'I hope you'll be able to do as well one day.'

'I hope so,' Charles answered gravely. 'I would like to write a poem, Papa.'

He was too shy to explain the thoughts that were clamouring for expression, and even if he tried he stuttered so badly that no one could understand him.

Books were more often his companions than people, but the books he found in Mr Salt's library were hardly suitable for a four-year-old. His vivid imagination gave him no peace and pictures he studied by day turned into dreams at night.

Culpepper's *Herbal* was harmless enough, with its pictures of plants and herbs, but it was dull compared with the *Great Book of Martyrs* and its tales of torture. The boy often pictured himself being burnt at the stake and liked to think he was brave enough not to mind.

He found Salmon's *Modern History* and stared fascinated at hideous Chinese gods and the great hooded serpent. But all these were as nothing compared with witches. They terrified him and drew him irresistibly at the same time – he was literally bewitched, searching for stories and pictures about them only to horrify himself the more.

He dreaded the dark, imagining he could see a witch on his pillow whenever he went into his room. He had a habit of turning his head so that he should not look at the horrid, leering thing.

It is not surprising that his dreams turned into night terrors and he regularly woke the household with his screams. Sometimes Mary went to him, feeling more than a little afraid herself, but more often it was Aunt Hetty who comforted him and lulled him back to sleep.

But suddenly she too turned into a witch. It happened when the terrified boy crept out of his bed one night to find her, longing for the comfort of her arms. It was not yet the adults' bed-time and he went to her room, whimpering and rubbing his knuckles into his sleepy eyes.

Her door was ajar and he saw his aunt sitting upright in her chair, with her eyes half open, her spectacles slipping down her nose as she nodded and dozed over her prayer book, mumbling the words as she read them.

She looked so strange in her old-fashioned dress that the boy stood rigid, his feet freezing to the oilcloth as he watched her lips silently moving.

'She's like the Witch of Endor – she's saying her prayers backwards! She must be a witch!' he thought. All the tales he had ever read about these mischief-making old women came crowding back into his mind and he held his breath as he looked again.

Aunt Hetty was still dozing and mumbling as he turned and fled back to his own room and dived under the bedclothes for protection where he lay shivering, half awake and half asleep until morning.

For several weeks after that he would stare at his aunt

in bewilderment until she wondered what he was about.

'Bless the child, why are you staring like that?' she asked more than once.

Charles longed to tell her of his dreadful fancies but could only stammer helplessly and run out of the room.

The night terrors grew worse and it was not long before the overwrought boy fell ill. A high fever left him so weak and pale that his mother became alarmed.

'Good country air,' the doctor said, 'that's what he needs most.'

Mrs Lamb thought for a moment.

'Mackery End is the place for him,' she said decisively, 'and Mary shall take him.'

2

Mackery End

Mrs Lamb lost no time in writing to her Aunt Gladman to ask if she would take Mary and Charles for a few weeks' holiday on the farm.

'What a blessing it is that I have such good relatives!' she remarked smugly as she sealed the letter.

'And such *superior* ones,' Aunt Hetty said sharply, 'that's what you meant to say, wasn't it?'

'I did not,' Mrs Lamb replied coldly, 'but you must

admit that the children would be very poorly off if they did not have *my* relations in Hertfordshire to go to.'

'Yes, yes,' Mr Lamb broke in to soothe the two ladies, 'they are very fortunate, my dear.'

'Oh, fortunate indeed!' snapped Aunt Hetty, 'they must be taught that their father's family is not good enough for them, that *some* people's manners need polishing!' This was a bitter reference to her sister-in-law's attempts to make a gentlewoman of her. 'There's no respect in this house, no respect at all!'

She stalked out of the room, rigid with indignation, and went to read Thomas à Kempis' *Devotional Course* in her own room.

Charles jumped up to follow her, sensing the antagonism between the two women, but his mother restrained him.

'Stay where you are and be quiet.'

'You'll like the farm, Charley,' his father said kindly. 'It'll bring the roses back to your cheeks.'

'I shall like it if Mary goes too.' He looked at his sister anxiously. He liked to be with her more than anyone else.

'Of course she's going! Now stop fidgeting!'

Later, when Mary took him for his favourite walk in the Temple Gardens he began to question her. She had stayed with Great-aunt Gladman more than once.

'What's Mackery End like, Mary? What is it the end of?'

'Nothing, as far as I know! What funny questions you ask, Charley!'

'But what is it like?' the little boy persisted.

'It's real country, with trees and flowers everywhere – even prettier than these gardens,' Mary tried to describe it, 'and the farm has every kind of animal.'

'Like Noah's Ark!'

'Not quite! But you'll soon see.'

Charles began to get excited and could hardly wait until the reply came to his mother's letter. He watched her face anxiously as she read it.

'You are to go,' she announced at length, 'but, mind, you're to behave well!'

Shouting with delight the boy rushed off to find Mary.

'M-Mary! M-Mary! Get ready, *quickly*! We're going to the farm!'

'Not yet, silly!' Mary smiled and gave him a hug. 'We can't walk there!'

Charles had to endure three long days of tensed-up excitement before they eventually set off to catch the stage coach from Fetter Lane. Mr and Mrs Lamb went with them to the Inn where the great coach waited amidst the bustle of passengers and their luggage.

'Now take care, and remember you are never to speak to strangers!' Mrs Lamb warned for the twentieth time.

'I'll watch 'em, ma'am, never fear,' the guard said gruffly. 'Here – set 'em down where I can keep me eye on 'em. There!'

The children settled, he drew up the steps as a sign that they were about to leave, then put his long horn to his lips and blew a mighty blast. The impatient, pawing horses were off at last and away they clattered down the narrow city street, the cumbersome vehicle lurching from side to side on the cobblestones. Mary and Charles turned to watch their parents, waving frantically until the coach turned a corner and took them out of sight. The journey had begun!

After the first excitement had worn off Mary began to feel hot and sick. She did not like coach journeys, but

Charles forgot the discomfort of the hard seat and the jolting of the wheels in the fascination of watching the guard.

Whenever they bowled through a town or village he would raise the horn as if he were a royal herald and play a lively little tune as the people waved them on.

The man smiled in a fatherly way at the round-eyed wonderment of the little boy.

'Like that tune, sonny? It's me own composition. I made it up, in a manner o' speaking.'

'That's very clever,' said Charles solemnly.

'Aye – you can do a lot wi' a coaching horn. Real good music you can make on 'em.'

They soon left the straggling outskirts of London behind and began to trot through winding country lanes at a steady even pace. Now and again, Charles would catch sight of some farm animals grazing peacefully in a field.

'Look, Mary – there's a cow! Over there!'

Mary glanced up disinterestedly. Her head was aching.

'Don't point, Charley! You just wait until you see Buttercup! She's the best cow of all!'

It was late afternoon by the time they reached Harpenden and the coach drew in to the Inn yard with a great flourish.

Mary opened her eyes with an effort.

'Come along, little missie,' the guard was saying, 'yer Ma said you was to get off 'ere.'

'Yes, I know, thank you,' Mary said, mustering her dignity.

The friendly guard lifted Charles down, then helped Mary, setting their luggage at their feet.

A burly red-faced farmer came out of the Inn and smiled as he saw the two forlorn children.

'Well, well, so you've got here safely and no mishaps!' he greeted them cheerily.

'Yes, thank you,' Mary replied, then turned to the guard politely. 'This is my great-uncle, come to meet us. Thank you for looking after us.'

Great-uncle Gladman felt in his pocket and a piece of silver changed hands as the guard touched his hat and left them.

'Come along, I've got the trap here.' Their uncle swung the bags on to his broad shoulders as neatly as if they were a sack of potatoes. 'We'll soon get you home now. I'll warrant you're both tired.'

He looked down into their peaky little faces sympathetically, but Charles was dumb with shyness.

The sturdy little pony set off at a brisk trot through the narrow country lanes. The spring hedgerows were aflame with blossom and a passing shower had left pearly dewdrops glistening on the leaves. The earth smelt sweet and clean and all the world was bright with promise of summer.

'This is *real* country!' the little boy cried, forgetting his shyness in the wonder of the discovery. 'There are flowers and trees everywhere, and the birds are so happy they're singing!'

His uncle chuckled. 'Aye, this is better than your old London any day!'

Mackery End Farm was barely three miles from Harpenden and the pony, thinking of the feed awaiting him, covered the distance in record time.

When the creeper-clad farmhouse came in sight Mary thought it looked as solid and reliable as Great-uncle Gladman himself.

The children's great-aunt was at the door to greet them,

her rosy face ashine with welcome. She hurried down the steps to lift Charles from the trap and the feel of her strong arms comforted the shy, nervous child.

'You poor mites – you must be tired and hungry after that long journey!' She set Charles down and looked at him, puzzled by his lack of response.

'Why, Charley, what's the matter? Don't you remember me?'

'N-no, ma'am,' the boy stammered, flushing painfully.

'Well, now! And to think I was in London only a few months ago! He was so fond of me then!'

'He was only little, Auntie,' Mary broke in, 'I expect he has forgotten.'

'Perhaps so,' his aunt said disappointedly.

'He'll soon learn to love you again – I know he will!' Mary gave her aunt a sweet, gentle smile which completely melted that good lady's heart.

'Never mind. Come and have tea, and you shall tell me how everyone is at the Temple.'

Chatting comfortably, she took them into the spacious farmhouse and set them down to an enormous tea of fresh country ham and eggs, home-made bread and spicy cakes. Even Charles' poor appetite was stimulated and they both ate with great enjoyment.

'You must go to bed early to-night,' Great-aunt Gladman beamed at them, 'and you can see the farm to-morrow. Take your brother upstairs, Mary, he's looking exhausted.'

Not even the hooting of the owls in the big oak tree disturbed the tired boy that night. Witches and their terrors were forgotten in the excitements of the day and seeing new places. Mary was thankful to sleep without being roused by screams in the small hours.

Charles was awakened early next morning by the song of the birds and the clatter of milk churns being wheeled out of the dairy. He stole into his sister's room and shook her gently.

'Wake up, Mary! It's to-morrow, and you promised to show me the farm!'

Mary blinked and yawned as she pushed the long dark hair out of her eyes.

'I *am* awake! O-o-oh, isn't it lovely? We're at Mackery End!' She felt free and happy. The Temple and all its restrictions seemed very far away.

They dressed quickly and went down to breakfast in the big stone-flagged kitchen. His aunt watched Charles as he spooned up porridge and cream with great relish.

'We'll soon make you big and strong at this rate,' she said with satisfaction. 'Now, get along, the pair of you, and get all the fresh air you can, but don't get into mischief.' She was hanging a fresh ham in the chimney corner as she spoke. 'Mary, show your brother the farmyard. He'll like the little chicks, I don't doubt.'

'Please, I want to see Buttercup,' Charles stammered shyly.

'You won't see her till she comes in for milking,' his aunt said. 'Emmie will let you see her then.'

That first morning nearly brought disaster to all Mary's hopes for her brother's recovery. It was a warm, sunny day and the children began to explore delightedly. But Charles suddenly paused, staring at the big black barn.

'Is that a witch's house?' he asked doubtfully.

'Of course not! It's where Uncle stores the corn. Come and see!'

Mary took the boy's hand and they peeped inside the barn rather breathlessly.

It was dim and a little eerie after the brilliance of the sunshine outside and Charles felt a sudden stab of fear as he saw a big, black-bearded man in the depths of the shadows. He started to beat the floor with a great stick and the noise was so dreadful that the little boy dragged his hand away from his sister's and ran away blindly, terrified of what he had seen.

Mary caught up with him as he reached the vegetable garden.

'You little silly!' she panted, 'why did you do that?'

'T-that man – I d-don't like him!'

'Why, that's only Will Tasker and he wouldn't hurt a fly! He's a very good-natured man.'

'He's not! He's hitting the floor!'

'That's because it's the threshing floor, silly, and he's beating out the corn so that the grain is separated from the straw. That stick is called a flail – it's the proper thing to use. Great-uncle will tell you if you ask him.'

Charles was only half convinced, but he allowed Mary to lead him back to the barn where he took another fearful peep round the door.

Will Tasker looked up and the black beard parted in a grin.

'Come on in, young ma-aster! I 'on't eat ye!'

But the sight of the bristly beard and the noise of the great flail as he continued to beat the corn were too much for Charles. He would have run away again if Mary had not clung to him.

'Let's go and see the chickens,' she said to pacify him.

The hens were feeding all over the yard and the prettiest little yellow chicks were clustering round a clucking bird who led them away from the children with a great show of agitation.

'Look, Charley, there are some baby ducklings and they've got a hen for a mother!' Mary cried. 'See how she's fussing because they want to go on the pond!'

Charles forgot his fears of Will Tasker as he watched the downy little ducklings take to the water.

'Silly bird!' he said, as the hen ran round the edge of the pond in a terrible state of agitation.

'She doesn't know she's got a brood of ducklings instead of chicks!' Mary pointed out. 'How easy it is to deceive a hen!'

As they wandered round the farm Mary was careful to show her brother only the good-tempered animals. She dreaded a return of the night terrors when they were so far from home.

At last it was milking time and they watched the herd of cows plod slowly to the big shed where the dairy maids waited with their stools and buckets ready.

'Cows are clever. Each one knows just where she is to go,' Mary said.

'Show me Buttercup! You promised to show me Buttercup!' The small boy jumped up and down in his impatience.

'We'll ask Emmie.'

Emmie, a big, fair-haired lass with sleeves rolled up to her elbows, invited the children to watch the milking.

'This 'ere's Buttercup,' she said fondly as she set her stool down by a mild-looking pied cow. 'You can stroke her, if you like. She won't mind.'

'O-oh! Isn't she l-lovely!' Charles reached up timidly and patted the gentle beast. Buttercup moved her head slowly, looking down at him with big liquid brown eyes, as if thanking him for his caress. The little boy grew bolder and stroked her again.

'I like Buttercup!' he announced proudly.

The milking over, they followed Emmie into the dairy and watched her fill the big pans with milk and cream.

'Doesn't it shine?' Mary said with admiration as she looked round the cool, clean dairy. 'It smells so nice too.'

'Ah – the missis'd 'ave me skin if it didn't!' Emmie laughed, showing strong white teeth in a sun-tanned face. 'I have to clean and scour from morn till night, but I do like to see my pans clean and bright.'

After that the children never missed a milking if they could help it and Charles always wanted to fondle Buttercup. New discoveries followed almost daily and although the countryside around was very beautiful, they still found the greatest pleasure in the farmyard.

On wet days they loved to play in the wood-house, which was really a large barn where wood was stored for the winter.

Charles was very excited when he first saw an egg lying neatly balanced on a pile of faggots.

'Be careful, or you'll break it!' Mary warned as he went to grab it. 'Look – there's another over there!' She gathered up her apron and put the eggs into it.

Their aunt was busily kneading bread as they took their find into the kitchen.

'The hens often lay in the wood-house and the eggs are hard to find sometimes,' she told them. 'You just keep an eye out for them and bring me as many as you can find, but mind, you're not to touch the wild birds' nests.'

Charles remembered this when a day or two later Will Tasker came into the kitchen, holding something carefully in his big rough hands.

'What have you got there?' Curiosity drove away his fear of the bearded giant.

'You come and see, Ma-aster Charley.'

Charles gave an exclamation of delight as he saw a perfect little birds' nest cradled in the man's hands. It held five pretty speckled eggs.

Great-aunt Gladman turned away from her cooking at the kitchen range. Her face was flushed as much with anger as with heat as she glared at the farmhand.

'What did I hear, Will Tasker?' She frowned at the nest. 'You'll take that straight back to where you found it, d'you hear? Tampering with wild birds! I won't have it!'

'Begging your pardon, ma'am, I fetched it for the little master here,' Will mumbled unhappily.

'Then he doesn't want it! A fine example you are! The birds won't sing again if their eggs are taken away!' Will backed to the door. 'Off with you! Put it back in the hedge and don't you ever do such a thing on this farm again!'

She watched the man cross the yard to the hedgerow beyond the garden and saw him replace the nest.

Charles thought he had never seen his kind aunt so angry before and felt a little afraid of her. Her face softened as she saw his distress.

'They'll be all right now, Charley. Maybe the birds won't have missed them.'

'B-but why may we take the hens' eggs and not those?' the boy was puzzled.

His aunt smiled and took him on her knee while she explained.

'A hen's different. She's a hospitable bird, she always lays more eggs than she wants on purpose to give some to her mistress to make puddings and custards with. That's why she always lives in the farmyard.'

Charles was satisfied and soon slipped off his aunt's knee and went into the garden to listen to the birds singing. It would have been terrible if Will Tasker had stopped them!

Life on the farm was very busy and very cheerful and Mary and Charles loved every minute of it. Looking for eggs became one of their favourite pastimes and the little boy loved seeing his aunt's broad smile when he gave her a lapful. Sometimes he found a few violets which she loved and let him put them in an eggcup full of water on the kitchen window sill.

The children were occasionally allowed to stay up for supper as a special treat. Then they would see the men come in from the fields and sit down at the long white tables in the kitchen, filling the old house with cheery talk and laughter.

Just before they came in a large faggot was flung on the fire and the wood crackled and blazed merrily, giving off a delightful smell of fields and woods. Then the crickets would begin to sing and the old shepherd would come in and take his place in the chimney corner, even after the hottest day in summer. It was a seat within the fireplace where the bacon hung over his head and the milk was suspended in a skillet over the fire.

'You shall be at the sheep-shearing supper,' Great-aunt Gladman promised her niece and nephew.

'When is sheep-shearing?' Mary asked at once.

'When the currants and gooseberries are ripe,' she was told.

It was a warm summer and they watched the fruit grow rosy and ripe in the sunshine.

'I wish it would hurry!' Charles often said. It seemed as slow as the sundial in the Temple!

B

At last the gooseberries were all picked and the time of the sheep-shearing drew near.

'You shall help me prepare for the big supper,' her aunt told Mary. 'I need an extra pair of hands.'

The two town children thought they had never seen such enormous plum-puddings being made, and while Mary helped to wash the fruit and chop the peel Charles gave an occasional stir.

'It's just like Christmas!' he said happily.

'Ah – and it's nearly as good as a harvest home supper, but not quite,' said their aunt.

When sheep shearing started Mary and Charles took their place at the orchard gate so that they could watch the sheep being driven in from the fields.

'Are they frightened?' asked Charles anxiously.

'No – they know the shepherd and he knows them. Watch how well they obey him,' Mary replied.

The docile sheep stood about under the trees, waiting their turn to be clipped. The children watched, fascinated, as the first ones were shorn of their thick wool. It lay about in little heaps, like clouds fallen out of the sky, thought the imaginative boy.

'Oh, don't they look clean and white!' Mary cried.

'Yes, but they're c-cold! Look, they're shivering!' Charles was concerned for the poor sheep.

'They'll be all right and their wool will begin to grow again very quickly.'

Lunch-time soon came round and the men sat under the trees in the orchard, eating great hunks of bread and cheese which they sliced with a clasp knife, while Farmer Gladman brought round tankards of ale.

'A-ah, this be thirsty work, ma-aster,' they said, raising their tankards to him in a toast.

As the day wore on the smell of roasting beef wafted out from the kitchen, putting an edge on everyone's appetite.

At last the work was done and it was time for the feasting. Great-aunt Gladman and the kitchen maids had been busy all day and what a feast they had prepared!

Charles' mouth watered as he looked at the great sizzling joints, the enormous bowls full of steaming vegetables, the cheeses just out of their muslins, the crisp new bread straight from the oven, the pies and the patties and the bowls of rich cream with mounds of fresh fruit.

'You might never see such another sheep-shearing!' Great-aunt Gladman said to the boy, 'so just you tuck in and enjoy it!'

Farmer Gladman led the company in from the fields and they were soon joined by the rosy-cheeked dairy maids, looking fresh and pretty in new print dresses. Then all the other servants came in and took their places at the long oak table, newly polished for the occasion. For once the old shepherd was persuaded to leave his chimney corner and take the place of honour beside the master. Charles and Mary sat one each side of their great-aunt and bowed their heads reverently as their uncle said grace.

Then the carving began and plates were passed to and fro to be filled. Tankards were filled with ale and the merrymaking began.

Charles could hardly eat the tasty morsels his aunt had saved for him for watching the company. Will Tasker was eating at a tremendous rate, his black beard going up and down in time with the champing of his jaws. Now and again he'd stop and let out a great bellow of laughter, then tip up his tankard and drain it with one grand gulp, afterwards wiping his mouth with the back of his hand.

'I think Will is very hungry and thirsty,' said Charles, in an awed voice.

Emmie was looking very pretty and coy beside a young cowman who was openly admiring her. Farmer Gladman was encouraging everyone to 'Eat up! There's plenty more where this came from!'

Soon someone got up to light the lamps and the big moths fluttered in at the open door.

'It's getting late,' Great-aunt Gladman said at length. 'You must take Charley up to bed, Mary.'

'Oh dear, it's been so *lovely*!' Mary sighed and gave her aunt a shy little kiss of thanks.

There were many friendly calls of 'Good night!' as the children went upstairs, Mary carrying their lighted candles.

'Oh, hasn't it been an exciting day?' she said happily, and Charles gave a sleepy nod, too tired to say anything.

But sleep would not come easily. Long after he lay in his bed he could hear the laughter and the talking, and then the singing which started as soon as the meal was ended. The boy sat up, straining his ears to catch the words, but they sounded like so much gibberish to him. When at last he fell asleep it was to the sound of a fiddle playing a merry jig.

When the time came for them to return home Charles had learned to love Mackery End so much that he was reluctant to leave it.

'Great-aunt Gladman has made you strong and well again, Charley,' Mary said persuasively, 'and now Mama wants us to go home before winter sets in.'

'I want to stay with Aunt and Emmie and Will,' the small boy protested miserably. Will Tasker had by now become his greatest friend.

'You may come again, as often as you like,' said Great-aunt Gladman cheerfully.

So with many tears of farewell Mary and Charles set off in the pony trap one early autumn morning to catch the stage coach at Harpenden. Will Tasker ran after the trap and thrust a new whistle into Charles' hand.

'I just carved it for ye,' he explained with a wide grin.

Charles clutched it tightly all the way home to the Temple, feeling as if he had a part of Mackery End with him.

Back in his own little room he carefully stowed it away among his treasures, to be looked at when he was quite alone.

3

First School and First Play

Soon after the visit to Mackery End his parents decided that Charles should go to school.

'Looking at books is all very well, but he'll never learn properly this way.' Mrs Lamb sat very stiff and upright in her chair as she sewed Mr Salt's shirt cuff. 'It's time he got some order into his mind.'

John Lamb chuckled as he looked at his youngest son sprawled upon the rug, completely absorbed in a large book.

'We've got a clever boy there, Elizabeth. Not many children know their letters before they can talk, and that's what our Charley did!'

'That was Mary's doing,' Mrs Lamb's mouth set in a firm line. 'He must be educated – like a gentleman.'

Her husband's merry eyes twinkled. 'It's as you say, my dear. After all, he's half a Field, isn't he?' He walked to the window and peered out to the terrace where a few Benchers strolled in earnest conversation. 'Shall we send him to Mrs Reynolds? She will not be too hard on him.'

'Mrs Reynolds – ?'

'You remember her. She used to live here in the Temple with her father. She was Miss Chambers then. She keeps a little school off Fleet Street now – the boy will learn to read there.'

Charles had caught the last few words and looked up indignantly. C620235

'But I *can* read, Papa! Mary taught me. Why must I learn?'

His father laughed indulgently. 'A good question, Charley, and the answer is you must start at the beginning.' He pointed to the open history book on the floor. 'That way you're trying to start at the top. School will be good for you.'

'School?' the boy's small, pale face brightened, 'I believe I shall like school.' And he returned to his book, lost to further conversation.

'I hope Mrs Reynolds is a *lady*, John.' Mrs Lamb lowered her voice.

The little man's lips twitched in amusement. 'As genteel as you are yourself, my dear, and to hear her speak you'd think you were sisters!'

Mrs Lamb, though she was well aware of her husband's

irrepressible sense of fun, appeared to be convinced and it was decided that Charles should go to Mrs Reynolds for his first lessons.

One Monday morning the little boy set off with Mary to enter the new strange world of school.

'What will school be like?' he asked his sister eagerly.

'It will be exciting,' she told him, squeezing his small hand affectionately. 'You'll learn how to write as well as read.'

'Then I shall be able to put down what I'm thinking about!' He looked up at Mary, scanning her face closely. 'You'll help me, Mary, won't you?'

'Of course, Charley. I'll always help you,' she replied softly.

All too soon for the nervous boy they arrived at Mrs Reynolds' house where she was waiting to greet them. She was very tall and very fair – like an angel, Charles thought.

They knew there was no Mr Reynolds about – where he had gone was a mystery, but it was probably the reason why she had to earn a living in a genteel, discreet way, giving simple instruction to a few select pupils. She was very glad to have little Charles Lamb. He was such an amiable, gentle boy and quite clever, she'd heard.

She gently disengaged his hand from Mary's. 'You're going to like it here, aren't you, Charles?'

'Y-yes, ma'am,' he stammered doubtfully. As he was led away from Mary he blinked away the tears.

He looked so small and fragile beside the tall Mrs Reynolds, but he was not so ill-looking since he had come back from the country, Mary comforted herself. The fresh air and farmhouse food had given him back his health after that long and dreadful illness but he still needed so much care and understanding. There were tears in her own eyes as she turned back towards the Temple. Mama would be waiting for her to help in Mr Salt's chambers.

On the whole Charles liked his school fellows although they made little impression on him. He was used to the company of adults and felt strange with other children.

They were mostly five and six-year-olds – too young to notice how badly the new boy stammered and too much under Mrs Reynolds' sharp eye to make fun of him if they had.

Charles avoided them as much as possible and attached himself to the teacher and soon made a discovery which sealed their friendship for ever.

'Have you heard of Oliver Goldsmith, Charles?' she asked one day when the boy lingered behind to look at a book.

'Oh, yes, ma'am! Papa told me he wrote some beautiful stories!' The intelligent eyes lit up.

'Do you know, he was a friend of mine!'

'A friend?' Charles looked at his teacher with awe. A friend of a great writer!

'Yes, he actually let me read his poem *The Deserted Village* in his own copy. It was wonderful!' Mrs Reynolds reminisced, quite forgetting that her attentive listener was not yet six years old.

Charles remembered having heard that Dr Goldsmith was buried in the Temple Churchyard and when he was walking through there with Mary he told her about it.

The two children began to read the tombstones, extolling the virtues of the departed, and the boy looked thoughtful.

'Mary,' he asked presently, 'where are the *naughty* people buried?'

'I don't know,' Mary answered seriously, 'and I don't think I want to find out.'

Charles thought the churchyard was somehow sad.

'Let's look at the river,' he urged, 'I like that best of all.'

It was a bright summer's day and they turned their footsteps to Fountain Court, lingering awhile to watch the play of the fountain.

'It's nice and shady here,' Mary said, glad to escape from the morbid atmosphere of the tombs.

The little boy touched the mechanism of the fountain with an exploratory finger and watched fascinated as the water rose in a graceful cascade.

'It's like magic!' he laughed, brushing the splashes from his face.

Mary entered into his mood. 'The sun has turned it into silver! Silver and diamonds! Aren't we rich?'

She glanced down Garden Court where the river lapped at the foot of the quiet Temple garden. 'The river looks like silver, too.'

'Perhaps that's been magic-ed!' Charles turned and ran down the Court and into the spacious garden. He loved the cool green lawns and the roses making such a splash of colour against the sombre background of the old buildings. He threw himself down upon the soft turf, watching the ripple and sparkle of the ever-moving water. He cupped his chin in his hands and began to dream.

'Get up, Charley,' Mary said crossly. 'You'll catch a chill, then Mama will blame me.'

With a sigh the boy got up, his dream world shattered.

He was content to spend his days like this, between school and the Temple, but life was already opening up and offering new experiences to the impressionable child.

Occasionally he was taken to see his godfather, a god-like person named Francis Fielde, and it was one of these visits that Charles was to remember for the rest of his life.

It was a cold November day when Mrs Lamb set out with her youngest son in the direction of High Holborn.

'Mind you answer up properly when your godfather speaks to you,' she said sharply as they hurried along Chancery Lane. 'You're half asleep most of the time! I'm sure I don't know what he thinks of you.'

Charles knew it was useless to answer his mother when she was in this mood and he soon became absorbed in the shops they were passing. The law stationers fascinated him most of all, the books and papers in the small windows looked so dusty that he wondered if anyone ever bought them. Now and again a shop door would open and a queer, musty smell would come out, reminding him of the lawyers' chambers in the Temple. Farther along there were glimpses of stately gardens behind great iron gates, and the majestic portals of Lincoln's Inn looked like the entrance to a fabulous castle.

All too soon they came to Featherstone Buildings, where Francis Fielde kept the oil shop on the corner. It was dark and mysterious inside the shop and Charles clung to his mother's hand a little more tightly.

A tall, grave-looking man came forward to meet them. He was so dignified that it was difficult to remember that he was an oilman. Indeed, he looked and spoke like one of the actors that he admired so tremendously.

'My dear Mrs Lamb, this is indeed a pleasure!' he extended his hand with a grand gesture and his small godson looked up in awe.

They were invited to sit down in a small back office where the smell of paraffin was almost overpowering.

Fielde patted Charles on the head benignly. 'And how are you getting on with your studies, boy?' He took a pride in his clever godson.

Charles stammered painfully, 'V-very w-well, sir, thank you.'

'Excellent! Excellent!' Mr Fielde felt that this reflected considerable credit on himself. 'And what books are you delving into this time, eh?'

'I l-like looking at the *Universal History*, sir, and Mr Salt lets me read his *Shakespeare* – '

'Shakespeare, eh?' Fielde was mightily pleased. 'Capital – capital!' He peered down at the boy intently. 'Do you want to be an actor, boy?'

'Oh, mercy me, no!' Mrs Lamb broke in hastily. 'He's got quite enough fancies in his head as it is. I hope he'll be a clerk, like his brother, and earn a steady wage.'

The boy looked from one to the other, his large dark eyes full of mute appeal. How could he tell them of the visions and dreams he conjured up in his mind and the beautiful words he wanted to write? There were still the nightmares, too – vivid and horrifying.

'He'll be leaving Mrs Reynolds' soon,' his mother went on, over his head. 'He's going to Mr Bird's.'

'Ha! Bird's a capital fellow, so I hear. The boy will do well enough there.'

Charles did not want to leave Mrs Reynolds' and said so.

'Nonsense!' his godfather said briskly. 'You're getting too big for a dame school.' He turned to Mrs Lamb. 'It's high time he saw a few plays – he needs bringing on.'

Mrs Lamb stiffened. 'Plays? We can't afford plays!'

'I'll send you some pit orders. Brinsley lets me have all I want.'

'Do you mean Sheridan?' Mrs Lamb was incredulous.

'Of course – none other! Great friend of mine – he appreciates what I do for the theatre.' Fielde was pleased with the impression he had made. 'It's settled then. I send the orders, you take the boy. He'll like it.'

Mrs Lamb glanced at her son doubtfully. 'I'll see what his father says, but thank you all the same.'

Secretly she thought the theatre was a lot of high-flown nonsense but she did not want to offend her kinsman. He might leave his godson a good inheritance one day.

Charles could hardly wait to tell his father that evening. John Lamb was delighted and ruffled his small son's dark hair affectionately.

'A play, eh? And at Drury Lane! My, Charley, you'll love that!'

Charles drew closer to his father. Papa seemed to *understand*. A play would be like seeing a book – a story – come to life!

He was almost sick with apprehension until at last the promised pit orders arrived, sent by Francis Fielde's delivery boy with a courteous note requesting that they be used on the night specified – 1st December, 1780.

Mrs Lamb made one last condition. 'We can't go if it rains,' she said firmly.

John Lamb winked at his son and nodded reassuringly, but from that moment Charles watched the skies anxiously. Surely there couldn't be any rain up there – !

His hopes were shattered. Towards noon the first great drops splashed down from a leaden sky, like tear drops wrung from the small boy's heart. He knelt on the window seat, his face pressed anxiously against the glass of the tall narrow window, watching the ceaseless rain steadily fill up the puddles in the courtyard down below.

His breath misted the pane so that he had to wipe it clean with his sleeve and he could feel his heart beating up in his throat as he fixed his attention on the largest of the puddles.

'Oh, if only the puddles would keep still!' he stammered in distress. 'Papa said if they kept still it meant it had stopped raining!' His large dark eyes turned piteously to his sister and suddenly filled with tears.

Mary, sitting quietly at her sewing, left it for a moment to comfort her little brother.

'Don't look down at the puddles, Charley, look up at the sky! See – there's a break coming in the clouds. It'll stop soon.'

Charles obediently looked up but was soon staring at the fascinating puddle again, watching the little rings made by each drop of rain.

Suddenly it was still! He could see the reflection of the tall building opposite glistening in its depth like a magic castle. He watched for another breathless moment to make sure he hadn't dreamt it, then clambered down from his perch excitedly.

'M-Mary – it's stopped! It's really stopped!'

Mary smiled happily. 'I told you it would, didn't I?'

The boy ran to the door in a frenzy of excitement.

'Mama! Mama! The rain's stopped! Now can we go?'

Mrs Lamb bustled into the room and looked out of the window.

'I told you, Charley, we can go if it keeps fine. Now be quiet, do, or you'll make yourself sick.'

After what seemed hours of agonised anticipation, they set out, John Lamb in his best black suit and his wife in her best bonnet. Charles walked quietly between his parents, dreading that even now some slight hitch should deprive him of this great treat. His observant eyes took in everything, the cheerful bustle of the London streets and the jostling crowds – were they all going to a theatre?

Around the theatre – Garrick's Drury, as it was called – the noise and excitement reached fever pitch. Smart carriages clattered up to the entrance and servants jumped down to make way for their masters. Coachmen called to each other and ragged urchins came out of the shadows, eager to hold the horses' heads for a copper or two. But this entrance was not for the Lambs. They made their way to an open doorway at the side and there they waited under shelter until another inner door should be opened. Charles looked round, wide-eyed and wondering at all the unfamiliar sights and sounds. He tried to make out the cries of the girls selling fruit.

''chase some oranges, 'chase some numparels, 'chase a bill of the play!' they called ceaselessly.

The boy tugged at his father's hand. 'What's a numparel?'

'Nonpareil,' his father corrected. 'It's a kind of apple. Would you like one?'

'No, thank you,' Charles was much too excited to eat.

He could see that inner door opening at last and the crowd began to pour in.

The Lambs chose seats with a good view of the stage and the boy sat between his parents, his small, thin legs dangling in mid-air. He looked around curiously. A green curtain hid the stage from sight. What was behind it? he wondered. Was it heaven?

The pictures painted on it reminded him of one of the pictures in Rowe's *Shakespeare*, the tent scene in *Troilus and Cressida*. How often he had looked at it! He studied it intently for a time, then wriggling in anticipation he whispered to his father, 'When will it begin, Papa?'

'Soon,' John Lamb smiled and pointed to the boxes lining the walls on the opposite side. 'Look at all the fine folk in the boxes, Charley. Aren't they grand?'

The boy transferred his fascinated stare from the curtains to the boxes and thought he had never seen such magnificence before.

'What a lot of jewellery they've got on!' he said, 'and, look, Papa! They've even got servants to wait on them!'

'That's right – flunkeys, they're called.'

The boxes looked very rich, upholstered in red plush, each one like a little room in itself, but what caught the boy's imagination were the splendid marble pilasters, decorated with some glistening material. Why, it looked just like sugar candy!

The orchestra lights went on and shed a gentle, soft radiance round the musicians' stands.

'That's your godfather Fielde's oil in those lamps,' Mrs Lamb said proudly.

A bell clanged harshly and Charles' small body tensed in delighted anticipation. Surely something would happen now? A minute, two minutes dragged on as before and the boy could bear no more. He suddenly hid his face in his mother's lap – that green curtain would *never* go up!

He kept his face muffled in the comforting black folds of his mother's dress until a second bell startled him.

'Get up now, Charley,' his mother gave him a gentle shake, 'you won't see the play.'

The play! He was up in a second, watching round-eyed as that tantalising curtain slowly disappeared. He caught his breath in wonder at the scene that was revealed on the stage and slid half off his seat, completely spellbound.

It was the first scene of the opera *Artaxerxes*, by Thomas Augustine Arne, and Charles Lamb was not yet six!

No wonder he hardly understood the action that was going on but he feasted his eyes on the vision.

'Know what it is, Charley?' his father whispered under cover of the music. 'It's Persia – the royal court.'

The boy had dabbled a good deal in the *Universal History* and knew what he was looking at. He heard the word Darius and immediately was in the midst of Daniel.

Gorgeous vestments, gardens, palaces and princesses passed before him in all their splendour as he sat motionless, lost in an enchanted dream. The brilliant colours were like the pictures in his book.

'It was a *real* book!' he tried to explain to Mary afterwards, 'all the people in it had come alive!'

Opera was followed by Harlequin's Invasion and Charles watched the historic buffoonery with the same grave attention, but it did not stir his imagination in the same way.

He was too young and too full of this exciting new experience to be critical but a great love of the theatre was born in him that night.

'Well, Charles, how did you like it?' said his father on the way home.

The boy was tired and overwrought. Impressions came crowding back on him as he stammered inadequately, 'It was l-lovely, thank you, Papa.'

That night his dreams were not of witches but of kings and princesses, passing in colourful procession before him, and they were all smiling.

4

The Magic of Blakesware

Soon after his sixth birthday Charles was sent to the
Academy of Mr William Bird, who described himself
grandly as an 'eminent writer and teacher of languages
and mathematics'.

It was, in fact, a humble day school where reading and
writing were taught to boys in the morning and to girls in
the evening. Mary Lamb had already been a pupil there,

46

so Charles did not feel such a stranger as he walked to Fetter Lane on that first morning.

The school was in a dingy little place called Bond Stables and the boy had to muster all his courage as he pushed the door and walked into the gloomy hall. It was bare save for rows of coat hooks on each wall and a satchel slung untidily in one corner.

A freckle-faced boy appeared from nowhere and looked at the small newcomer, standing alone and uncertain.

'Hullo! Who are you? New boy?'

Charles nodded dumbly and the boy was soon joined by others, all curious and staring.

'What's your name, new boy?'

'C-Charles L-Lamb!' The nervous boy stammered more than usual.

'O-oh! C-C-Charles L-L-Lamb!' the boys mimicked in chorus, imitating Charles' painful facial contortions.

The boy turned away to hide the tears that sprang to his eyes. Why had his parents sent him to such a cruel place?

The tormenting stopped abruptly as Mr Bird emerged from a door on the right.

He was a squat, corpulent man who looked like some weird Eastern potentate in a gaudy flowered Indian gown.

'And what, if I may enquire, is the cause of all this noise?' he asked with a mildness which did not deceive the culprits.

They looked to their leader, Tom Watson, to answer.

'We – we were talking to the new boy, sir,' he faltered.

'*Talking*, eh?' Bird's tone grew even softer and milder. 'Well, I'll talk to you later and see if I can teach you manners.' His brightly coloured gown flapped menacingly and Charles was reminded of an exotic prehistoric bird that he had seen in a book. 'Now, *go*!' the master suddenly thundered, 'before I flay you alive!'

The terrified boys scuttled away, into the schoolroom, and Mr Bird beckoned to Charles.

'Come here, boy, and let's take a look at you. You're Charles Lamb, aren't you?'

'Y-yes, s-sir.' The boy followed the grotesque figure of the headmaster into his study.

It was a small and dingy room, where the chief furnishings were a rickety bookcase with shelves bowed with the weight of heavy, unused volumes, a large, ink-stained desk behind which was an imposing swivel chair, but what riveted Charles' attention most of all was the terrible array of canes on the wall, carefully arranged like a display of treasures.

Was this a torture chamber?

A lean, lanky young man with straight sandy hair was busy filling an inkwell at the desk, making a few more blots in the process. He looked at the small frightened boy and nodded.

'Ah, Mr Cook,' said Mr Bird grandly, 'this is the new boy, Lamb.' They glanced at each other with secret satisfaction. A new boy meant another fee. 'Pay special attention to his writing, please.'

'I will, Uncle,' Mr Cook replied cheerfully.

'And don't "Uncle" me in front of the boys!' Mr Bird said testily. 'How many more times must I tell you?'

'Sorry, *sir*,' his nephew grinned imperturbably, then turned to Charles. 'Come with me, youngster.'

He led the way into the schoolroom where Charles' recent tormentors were already seated, legs firmly wedged into uncomfortable sloping desks. The boy thought that the sunken leaden inkstands looked just like another row of blots to add to those which already covered the battered desks.

No one dared to look up as the new boy entered.

'Sit here,' Mr Cook indicated a seat at the end of a row and Charles obediently slid in beside a fair-haired boy who looked round with a sly grin.

'Can you do pot hooks and hangers, boy?' Mr Cook asked.

'Oh, y-yes, sir, v-very well!'

Charles heard a muttered 'Swank!' from his neighbour and coloured violently.

Mr Cook cuffed the offender and went on, 'Good! Now you must learn to write a free hand – like this.'

The master wrote some letters slowly and painstakingly, which Charles secretly thought was play for babies, but already he had seen enough to know when to keep his thoughts to himself.

The boy began to copy the letters and Mr Cook moved away and sat behind a high desk, where he could see the whole of the room at a glance.

He called the names of his pupils, ticking each one off in the register in front of him, then added Charles Lamb in his large flowing script. He closed the book and carefully arranged a ferule in front of him.

Charles looked on curiously, wondering what use the thing had. It looked like a flat ruler widening into a pear shape at one end with a hole in the middle, rather like a cupping glass.

'What's that?' he whispered to his neighbour.

'That's what you get when you make too many mistakes, or talk too much,' the boy answered. 'I had it yesterday. Look – it makes blisters!'

He held out his left hand under cover of the desk and

there was a big blister in the middle of the palm. Charles looked at it with a horrid fascination.

'It's – it's *torture* – !' he began, then quickly subsided as the master glared at him. He had no wish to sample that wicked-looking instrument for himself.

He turned back to his work but it was difficult to form his letters well with the boy next to him elbowing him out of his seat. But he dared not complain – he had no doubt now that there was a torture chamber somewhere in the house!

The simple exercises did not interest him but he found a certain satisfaction in watching his clean fingers darken with ink as the morning wore on. At least this was better than Mrs Reynolds' scratchy slates – it made him feel much more important.

By glancing sideways Charles discovered that he could just see through a window a drab little garden in the passage leading from Fetter Lane into Bartlett's Buildings. It was dusty and neglected but to the imprisoned boy it looked like the Garden of Allah. He thought the morning would never end and he wanted more than anything to get out there by himself, away from these hostile boys and the cruel masters.

At last he was free and ran home as if the three winged Furies were after him. He ran down Fleet Street without pausing, but as he got near St Dunstan's Church he saw that the clock was about to strike. He waited, breathless, as the figures of the two giants prepared to raise their iron clubs and hammer out the hours. Boom! went the first stroke, and the boy watched, entranced, wondering why the clock face didn't break under the repeated blows, but somehow it went on, none the worse for the giants' onslaught each hour.

He had seen the clock strike a hundred times before, and now the familiar sight comforted him and helped him to shake off the nightmarish feeling his new school had given him.

'Well, my boy, what have you learnt today?' his father asked that evening.

The boy's small thin face grew scornful.

'Nothing! I know it already, Papa. I'd rather read Mr Salt's books, please.'

John Lamb glanced at his wife with pride.

'What did I tell you, Elizabeth? He's ahead of all the others, you see.'

'That's as may be,' Mrs Lamb answered repressively, 'but there's no need to put ideas into the boy's head. He's got plenty to learn yet.'

Charles found few friends at this school. The fair-haired boy, whose name was William, helped him to avoid trouble.

'You get a whipping from Mr Bird if you do anything bad,' he warned, and grinned mischievously at Charles' look of horror.

'W-why does he do that?'

William looked surprised. 'You *are* green! All boys get whippings! Haven't you ever had any?'

'N-no,' Charles stammered, thinking of his kind Mrs Reynolds. He had never had more than a mild slap.

William laughed. 'You'll soon see what it's like, but mind you're not the one getting it! It hurts!' He held his behind and made mock grimaces of pain.

Charles saw, and heard, for himself a few days later when the irrepressible Tom Watson was called out by Mr Bird.

'Watson, you have been persistently lazy and untidy in

your work,' said the master in that peculiarly mild tone which the boys found so much more terrifying than his anger. 'You must be taught to pay attention, must you not? You will please to come into my study.'

The wretched boy, looking rather green, followed the gorgeously robed little master into the adjoining room. A few moments later the listening boys in the schoolroom heard a steady rhythmic swishing followed by Tom's howls.

Charles clutched William's arm in fright.

'Shut *up*!' hissed that boy, 'or you'll get it yourself!'

Charles put his hands over his ears and pressed hard to keep out the hateful sounds of suffering which his sensitive nature could not bear, and only removed them when William tugged at his sleeve and whispered contemptuously,

'It's all over now – *booby*!'

Tom Watson came back into the room, subdued and sniffing, and sat down with exaggerated care. Mr Bird followed, beaming upon the class benignly, as if he had just enjoyed a very pleasant interlude.

But on the whole these solemn whippings were not frequent and the blister-raising ferule was far more often in use.

Young Charles Lamb did nothing to merit these more drastic punishments and was so quick at learning that the easy-going Mr Cook left him to master copy writing alone.

The boy was filled with pride when he had completed his first copy, 'Art Improves Nature', in a bold, round hand.

He waited timidly for Mr Bird's judgment. Some of the boys had told him that those strange figures on the master's Indian gown were signs of pain and suffering and he turned his eyes away in dread.

'H'm. Good. Very good!' and Charles noted with relief that the master's tone was brusque without the dreaded mildness.

As the summer holidays drew near the boys' sidelong glances to the dusty little garden became more frequent and more longing. Charles longed to be free to visit his favourite haunts around the Temple with Mary.

Then Mrs Lamb announced that they were both to go to Grandmother Field at Blakesware for a holiday.

'You'll get plenty of fresh air and good food there, and your grandmother will instil a little order into you!' she said with a withering look at Mary, who looked pale and downcast.

Charles looked forward to the journey and fancied himself a seasoned traveller as they boarded the stage coach at Fetter Lane, but this time they were bound for Ware.

Mrs Field sent a groom with a pony trap to meet them. The man pointed out the familiar landmarks as they bowled through the country lanes and Charles jumped up and down in excitement as they came within sight of the house.

Blakesware House was an imposing family mansion set in several acres of grounds and it looked scarcely real to the city child.

'It looks like a palace, Mary! Is it a palace?'

'No, it's just a large country house,' Mary said, 'and it belongs to a family called Plumer.'

'Ah – but they've left it now, miss, and gone to live in a newer house out Widford way, more's the pity,' the groom put in.

'Fancy leaving all this!' Charles made a sweeping gesture as he looked round at the woods and parkland. 'I think they're silly!'

'No one wants the old place now,' the groom said sadly. 'There's just your grandmother here, looking after it, and a right good job she makes of it too!'

'Isn't she lonely all by herself?' asked the boy.

'Bless you, no! She's too busy to be lonely!' the man laughed good-naturedly as he turned the pony in through the great gates and across the wide courtyard. 'Finest dancer in the county she was at one time, or so I've heard tell, but now – ' he sighed, 'they don't even have servants' balls no more.'

The pony stopped at a side door and Grandmother Field came out to meet them. She was tall, upright and graceful and would easily have passed for the owner of the great house instead of the housekeeper.

She made her daughter's children very welcome and was glad of the opportunity to teach them the more superior ways of the Fields.

'Now, my dears,' she said after the first greetings were over, 'you may go where you like so long as you don't get into mischief, and remember your manners.'

Charles stammered out 'Y-yes, thank you, Grandmama.'

From the first moment of his arrival he was so fascinated with the house and its treasures that he felt as if he had stepped into another world. At the first opportunity he whispered to Mary, 'Let's explore!'

'All right. We'll begin with the downstairs rooms. I saw them once when I came with John.' Mary took her brother's hand and led him along a corridor at the end of which was a green baize door.

They pushed it open and found themselves in a vast

marble-paved hall. Round the walls hung the heads of twelve Caesars, stern and majestic in their dignity. Charles gave an exclamation of delight and dragged a chair to the nearest one.

'Be careful!' Mary warned as he clambered up to read the inscriptions beneath the heads.

'Perhaps Julius Caesar or Augustus really lived here once,' the boy said in awe, 'there might have been hundreds of slaves here too!'

'Of course there weren't! One of the Plumers built Blakesware House and collected all these things,' Mary said sensibly. 'Look at all these pictures by Hogarth — they're not Roman!'

But Charles preferred the Caesars to Hogarth and his attention was only diverted by Mary's discovery of a broken battledore and shuttlecock on a marble slab.

'Children must have lived here at some time,' she said softly, 'but their playthings were forgotten.'

'I wonder what they were like? Are they dead now, Mary?'

Charles put out a hand and touched the marble shoulder of a satyr. He shuddered at its icy touch but he had proved to himself that the hideous thing was not alive.

From the hall they wandered into a room full of family portraits and Charles stood entranced before the picture of a little girl with one arm round a lamb's neck and in her hand a large bunch of roses.

'Oh, isn't she pretty! She's one of the children who played in the hall — I know she is!' He smiled at the portrait as he spoke. 'Don't you wish she was our sister, Mary?'

Mary felt a twinge of jealousy as she saw her brother's rapt expression. 'No, I don't think I do. People are not always as nice as they look. Come away, Charley, there's a lot more to see yet.'

They roamed about the vast empty rooms, with worn-out hangings, fluttering tapestries and carved oaken panels, all telling a tale of departed splendour .

The best rooms were in perpetual gloom. Only a glimmer of light penetrated through the tops of the heavy window shutters and the furniture was perpetually shrouded in dust covers.

'Come and see this chimney piece, Charley,' Mary led her brother over to a fine carved mantel; 'it tells the story of the Children in the Wood and their Wicked Uncle. It's all supposed to have happened near here.'

They peered at it closely in the dimness and the boy put out a finger to trace the finely chiselled figures.

'I like the robins – I can feel the feathers!'

'That shows how well the craftsman carved them. They look almost real!'

While Charles was absorbed in the story told on the chimney piece, Mary peered under the dust covers to see the worked furniture and carpets. She loved fine needlework and was lost in admiration at the beauty of the intricate designs she saw.

'I've never seen anything as good as this!' she exclaimed. 'Grandmama said Mrs Plumer made nearly all her own covers and carpets! I wish I were as clever as that, but sometimes I feel so *muddled*!' The girl put her hand to her head in a tired gesture.

Charles heard the note of distress in her voice and said gravely, 'You *are* clever, Mary! I told Papa I really needn't go to school because you teach me much better than Mr Bird or Mr Cook. I would rather read books with you than anyone else in the world!'

Tears of gratitude came into Mary's soft brown eyes as she looked at her frail little brother, whose behaviour was so much older than his years. 'You are a dear, good boy, Charley. I hope God will be good to us and let us stay together always!'

'I expect He will.' The boy tried to think of something to comfort her. 'Let's look at some more needlework. You like that.'

'Oh, yes!' Mary jumped up at once. 'Come and see the tapestries in the bedrooms. They're so cleverly worked. It must have taken years to do them!'

She took Charles upstairs to the great silent rooms, where imposing four-posters were draped in dust sheets and heavy mahogany furniture concealed beneath covers.

'Is there a ghost?' Charles asked doubtfully.

'No!' Mary answered sharply. 'At least, I hope not. Let's hurry and look at the tapestries and go downstairs again.'

They went on tiptoe to examine the hangings and Charles was tense with excitement.

'Why, they're Bible people!'

'Yes, some of them are. See, there's Hagar, with Ishmael, her little boy, wandering in the wilderness.'

'Little Ishmael looks very pretty. I feel so sorry for him, Mary.'

The boy turned from Hagar's sad story to stare wide-eyed at a wild-looking monarch, with long fingers like birds' claws.

'That's Nebuchadnezzar when he had to eat grass,' Mary said, 'doesn't he look terrible?'

Both Ishmael and the grass-eating king were forgotten as Charles lifted a coverlet and came eye to eye with a stern bright face. As he gazed it seemed as if all the poems of Ovid came to life, vivid and enthralling. Greek gods and goddesses sported and fought their way around the walls. Here was Acteon – there was Diana – it was sheer enchantment to the boy to recognize his favourites of the classics in such never-ending glory.

As often as he could he would steal away by himself to dream away an hour or two in solitary bliss, living in a world of fantasy peopled with the gods from Olympus.

But his habits of dreaming often exasperated his grandmother.

'Don't mope about in corners like that, boy!' she would say impatiently when she came across her grandson gazing at the Caesars as if he would will them to come alive. 'Why, when your brother John stayed here he'd be off on the most mettlesome horse he could find in the stables and cover half the county in a morning! *And* he'd join the hunters when they were out and have a right good time! Ah, there was a handsome lad for you, and brave with it!'

Charles silently agreed that his brother was both brave and handsome but he knew he could no more be like him than a dog could be like a giraffe.

'He'd too much spirit to be cooped up here all day long!' the old lady finished irritably. 'Why can't you take a leaf out of his book? As for Polly, I don't know what those poor, crazy moithered brains of hers are thinking about half the time!'

Mary, so often bewildered by her grandmother's tirades, took Charles into the garden, to the friendly old wood which they had christened the Wilderness. Here they could talk without interference.

'I don't think Grandmama loves us, Mary,' Charles said sadly after one of these outbursts.

'Yes, she does. It's just her way,' Mary replied dutifully.

'Of course she likes John best. You know everyone does.'

The truth was, Grandmother Field was anxious to do her best for her daughter's family, especially when they were away from the influence of that too easy-going father of theirs, but her patience was apt to be strained at times.

The children learned to expect rough remedies at Blakesware and imagined the medicine chest to be full of instruments of torture. Mrs Field's rough and ready surgery when sewing up a cut finger was sheer torment and Saturday night's 'flannel' was almost as bad, when the old lady would screw up a piece of rough Witney blanket and thrust it into the corners of their eyes with soap that scoured and smarted.

'Nonsense! It doesn't hurt!' she would say briskly.

Charles never forgot the day a fly flew into his eye. He ran to his grandmother who was busy in the kitchen.

'Stop that wailing! We'll soon get that out!' she said sharply and proceeded to pound up about two ounces of the finest loaf sugar. 'Now sit down and open your eye as wide as you can.'

The boy did so, propping his eyelids open with his fingers. With a quick gesture his grandmother blew the whole of the contents of the paper in his eye.

Charles roared with pain and in the deluge of tears the fly was washed out.

'There, now,' Mrs Field said matter-of-factly, 'the fly is out!'

But in spite of this Spartan treatment Charles was happy. He loved to lie under the trees and dream as he watched the dappled sunlight dancing on the carpet of pine needles.

He made a friend of Ben, the gardener, whose soft speech and gentle smile won the boy's heart, but it was

Ben who unwittingly destroyed his secret kingdom under the downswept branches of the fir trees. He lopped off those magnificent lower limbs that touched the ground and the old trees were shorn of their majesty.

'L-look what you've done, Ben!' Charles raged when he discovered it, 'it's – it's like cutting off someone's arms!'

'Now, now, don't take on so, Master Charley,' said old Ben kindly. 'Trees have to be pruned or they won't grow beautiful.'

'But they *were* beautiful!' the small boy stormed, 'and – and they were my tent!'

He felt as if his dreams had been trampled on.

'Never you mind,' Ben patted the dark head gently, 'you just come along o' me to the fruit garden. Mebbe you'll like that.'

Charles wrenched his eyes away from his mutilated friends and followed Ben, hardly caring that this was a treat being offered him. They walked silently between the orderly rows of fruit, ripe for the plucking.

'There, now, you can pick and eat what you like, but don't go touchin' the wall fruit,' said the gardener as he moved away, 'and mind you don't go and give yourself the colly-wobbles or your Gran'll be out for my skin!'

The boy picked a few currants, then wiped his stained fingers on some leaves. He liked the pungent smell and sniffed appreciatively as he wandered along the path. He came to the sheltered south wall where the peaches and nectarines grew. A breeze stirred the leaves and a shaft of sunlight picked out a large ripe golden peach, flushed and rosy with the sun. It was the last one.

The boy did not like peaches, they were too rough to the tongue, but the temptation to pick and hold the lovely fruit was almost irresistible. He turned away, but a minute later he was back again, gazing and longing.

With a sudden burst of wilfulness he reached up and picked the peach. It was his! He could feel its downy, sun-warmed skin caressing his hand.

Suddenly the sun went in and a few drops of rain splashed on to his face and it was like a cold douche. He didn't *want* the peach! He threw it on to the ground as if it were a live coal and turned and ran down the path, leaving the luscious fruit to rot in the grass.

Hot with shame he ran into the garden and threw himself down by the fish pond, among the tall grasses and reeds. He watched the pretty little dace darting to and fro like silver spears, frisking and dancing as they chased the insects. The boy stiffened as he saw a great pike, almost invisible as it hung motionless in the weeds. It was waiting to catch the little dace! He stirred the water vigorously in the effort to dislodge it – the little fish should not be eaten by this ugly cannibal while he was there to prevent it!

The fish soon made him forget about the peach, but his conscience troubled him for days afterwards whenever he thought about it.

Charles spent many holidays at Blakesware after that and the magic never failed to work. He grew to love every nook and corner of the place, its freedom, the rich spaciousness of the house and grounds and the quiet beauty of the countryside. More than anything he loved his little room, where he could look through the small painted pane on a fine summer's morning on to a world of enchantment, where the sun turned the garden into Paradise and the birds sang from dawn to dusk.

The contrast between Blakesware and Mr Bird's

Academy was almost too great to be borne during the first days of his return, but when at the end of the year he was told that he had won the prize for the best spelling, everything else was put out of his head for the sheer joy of it.

Who cared now for those stupid, mimicking boys?

'My, Charley, you'll be a credit to us yet,' his father said exuberantly and Aunt Hetty nodded in agreement.

'But, mind, don't let it turn your head!' his mother warned, noticing the gleam of over-excitement in her son's eyes.

5

Bluecoat Boy

The wish to leave the dreary school in Fetter Lane came true sooner than Charles anticipated.

It was not long after he had won the spelling prize that his father came home with some important-looking papers in his hand.

'You're a lucky boy, Charley! Mr Yeates has got you a place in Christ's Hospital – the Bluecoat School. There!

What d'you think of that?' John Lamb seated himself at the table and spread the papers before him.

The boy came and stood at his elbow curiously.

'Am I to go to a new school, Papa?'

'Yes, and a very good school it is, by all accounts.'

The family were together in the sitting-room and it was nearly time for supper. Mrs Lamb put down her darning.

'Who is this Mr Yeates, John?'

'Why, my dear, he is a friend of Mr Salt's and he also happens to be a Governor of Christ's Hospital. You know Mr Salt has always said that Charley is worth a good education.'

'S'sh!' Mrs Lamb shot a warning glance towards the listening boy, 'we don't want any big opinions of ourselves, thank you!'

'All the same, it's a great opportunity for the boy. He'll get his fill of Greek and Latin there.'

'I suppose you know that Christ's Hospital is a religious foundation,' John remarked to his brother. 'You don't want to end up in the Church, Charley. There's more money in commerce.'

John was rather a dandified young man these days, earning a small salary as a clerk at the South Sea House, and his family looked on him with some awe.

'I want to learn Greek and Latin,' Charles insisted. He turned to his father eagerly. 'What is Christ's Hospital like, Papa? Is it a boarding school?'

'Oh, yes. Its real title is a Religious, Royal and Ancient Foundation,' the little man's eyes twinkled at his son, 'that's more important than an ordinary school, isn't it?'

'It sounds more like a Church!'

'It is where a monastery used to be before Henry VIII

dissolved it. It was called the House of the Grey Friars then. Edward VI made it into one of the Royal Hospitals to help poor people, but it's never really been a foundlings' hospital, or an orphanage, for that matter. It's a school for the children of parents who need – er – a little financial help in educating their families.'

'Are *we* poor, Papa?' Charles asked shrewdly.

Mrs Lamb clicked her tongue impatiently as her husband shuffled the papers of admission. He began to write his signature slowly and carefully before he replied.

'We're not rich, my boy, not by any means rich enough to give you the advantages you should have.'

'*He* doesn't need advantages – he'll take them for himself!' John scoffed.

Charles thought hard for a moment or two, then demanded,

'How many boys go to this school, Papa?'

'About six hundred.'

Charles whistled in surprise. 'Six hundred! When I go there will be six hundred and one!' He chuckled at the thought.

Mary, sitting quietly by the window to get the best light, dropped a tear on to her sewing. She dare not join in the family discussion, she would only be crushed by her mother. She could only think of how much she was going to miss her little brother. She had been looking forward to earning her own money as a professional dressmaker but even that lost its savour now that she knew Charles was to go away.

During the next few days brother and sister went many times into the City to gaze through the narrow Grey Friars' Gate in Newgate Street at the famous charity school. It was a majestic pile of buildings, grouped around large playgrounds and quiet cloisters where the monks used to walk. Charles looked curiously at the boys in their long blue coats, belted at the waist, with bright yellow stockings and black buckled shoes showing beneath them.

'They look like monks,' he remarked.

'But the little bands of white linen at the neck look more like a lawyer's bib,' Mary pointed out. 'It's a very picturesque dress, Charley, and I'm sure it must be warm.'

Once the beadle on duty at the gate warned them to keep their distance.

'I 'as job enough to keep these young limbs in and the street urchins out,' he grumbled, 'asides keepin' me eye on the public comin' and goin'. Look at 'em!' He waved his arm at the stream of people who seemed to be constantly using the right of way through the school grounds from Little Britain to Newgate Street. 'Bear garden ain't in it!'

'We're only looking,' Mary explained. 'My brother is going to be a pupil here.'

'Oh, *is* he! Then he'll be the other side o' this gate then and not before!' the man retorted.

It was early October when Charles was admitted to the school and put on his new 'blues' for the first time. He discovered that the traditional uniform also included a long yellow vest, breeches of Russian drab and a small blue cap which perched on his head like a crumpet.

He felt strange and self-conscious as a stout, red-faced beadle led him to the steward's room.

'Is this the headmaster?' the boy asked timidly.

'Lor' bless yer, no! You won't see a master round 'ere after lessons is done! Ho, no! This 'ere's the steward and he's top dog out o' school time, see? You mind your p's and q's when he's around, young shaver! In you go!'

The steward, all too conscious of his power, looked

down his long thin nose at the trembling small boy.

'You're Charles Lamb, aren't you?'

Charles could only stutter inarticulately.

'All right, don't have a fit, child! If you behave yourself you'll come to no harm. If you don't – ' he paused ominously, 'well, you'll see soon enough. I advise you not to try to run away, that's all. The punishment is very severe – *very* severe.' He looked the boy up and down critically. 'Mind you keep yourself clean and tidy – those clothes cost money. You're to wear them always, d'you hear? Even at home – if your people want you at home.'

Charles managed to stammer 'Y-yes, s-sir,' before the beadle took him out again, down a flight of stone steps to an outer door which led to the cloisters.

'My, my, we are tongue-tied, aren't we! Frightened, I'll say. But don't take on, sonny. You'll soon get used to it and be like all the other wicked young varmints. Now, you wait there till you hear the supper bell, then follow all the others in.'

He gave Charles a friendly push and left him in the shelter of the cloisters to watch his boisterous new schoolfellows at play. Most of them had their gowns rolled up and tucked into their girdles, the better to play leap-frog. Others were throwing balls about or whipping tops with great energy.

No one appeared to take any notice of the members of the public hurrying to and fro. After the quiet orderliness of the Temple the boy thought it sheer pandemonium.

'Hullo, young 'un!' Charles gave a jump as he heard a voice at his elbow. 'New boy, or I'm a Dutchman! Shake!'

He looked round to see a boy considerably bigger than himself, with a good-humoured face crowned by a mass of glossy black hair falling smoothly over his forehead.

Charles took the friendly hand held out to him.

'Are you n-new too?'

'Yes, at least I've just come from the Junior School at Hertford, but this is different. It's so *big*!' He sighed deeply and turned dark luminous eyes on Charles. 'My name's Coleridge – Samuel Taylor Coleridge. What's yours?'

'Charles Lamb.' Already the smaller boy's eyes were alight with hero-worship. To think that this big boy had spoken to him!

'Well, Charles Lamb, I hope we're going to survive the next few years. I doubt it, though.' Coleridge leant against a stone pillar gloomily. 'Where's your home?'

'I l-live in the Inner Temple, not far from here.'

'Some people have all the luck! And I bet one of the lawyers is your patron!'

Charles nodded, uncertain whether this was a good or bad thing to acknowledge.

'My people live in Devon,' Coleridge went on. 'My Pater's the Vicar of Ottery St Mary. It's too far away, and too expensive, for me to go home –' He turned his head aside so that the other should not see the homesickness that overwhelmed him. 'You're only a kid, aren't you? How old are you?'

'Seven and a half,' Charles answered proudly.

At this Coleridge looked more downcast than ever. 'I'm nearly ten. That means we shall be separated – put in different wards, I expect.'

'Wards?' Charles looked puzzled.

'Dormitories. They call them wards here and the women in charge of them are called nurses. Don't ask me why!'

There was a sudden scuffle at the gate as a beadle

dragged a boy back inside by the scruff of the neck.

'None o' these chasin' larks, me lad,' he roared, 'or I'll clap you in chains!'

'Chains?' Charles repeated horrified. 'That's what they do in prison!'

'They do it here, too. They told me what to expect at the other school,' Coleridge was slightly superior. 'It's the punishment for running away. The first time you're caught you're chained up in a cell. The second time you're shut in a dark dungeon all alone and beaten at odd intervals. The third time you get a public flogging and you're expelled.' He paused. 'Nice prospect, isn't it?'

'I shall *never* run away!' Charles shivered at the thought.

'I expect I shall be tempted to but I wouldn't know where to go,' Coleridge said miserably.

Just then the supper bell went and the two new boys followed the others who were making for the Great Hall.

Charles was lost in admiration at his first sight of this splendid eating room, which his father had told him was one of the noblest in England.

'It reminds me of the Temple,' he said excitedly to Coleridge, before they were separated by the crowd of boys.

He hardly heard what the nurse in charge of his table said to him, but automatically slid into place, his eyes riveted on the huge picture on the wall opposite him. Later, he learnt that it was as big as a cricket pitch, that it was painted by Verrio and showed King Charles II delivering the charter to the Royal Mathematical School.

Under the picture were an oaken pulpit with carved panels of the saints and a small gallery let into the wall for choir boys. His eyes strayed to another gallery at the north end where he could see the organ.

c*

It was all far too beautiful to be an ordinary school, the boy thought.

He listened with reverence as one of the tall, big boys read a passage from the Bible with practised ease, after which Charles was quick to follow the example of the other boys who knelt while grace was said, their monitors standing and facing them.

In this atmosphere of long-standing tradition and stately dignity a meagre meal of bread and cheese was apportioned out as if weighed and cut to the last half ounce.

'Phew! Only six o'clock and we go hungry until to-morrow's breakfast of bread and bad beer!' the boy next to Charles groaned as they rose from the table, appetites unappeased.

'I'm not hungry!' Charles protested.

'Wait till you've been here a week or two – you'll be *starving*!' the boy said disgustedly. 'Blue porridge, filthy mutton crags and pease soup like water! Ugh! And they try to poison you with gags!'

'Gags? What are they?'

'You *are* a greenhorn! They're whopping great lumps of fat – nobody eats them here. They're frightful!'

'That's enough, Thornton!' the stern-faced nurse pounced on them. 'Off to bed with you and show Charles Lamb where to go. He sleeps next to you.'

The boy, muttering under his breath, led the way out of the Great Hall.

'Come on – I'll show you where to wash first. You won't be able to dodge it,' he turned down a dank stone passageway. 'That's the wash-house down there,' he pointed to a dark place reeking of damp, 'but we only go in there when we bath, six at a time.'

'Six at a time!' Charles could hardly believe it.

'Yes, in one bath, *and* you'd better not turn up your nose! Look, this is where you wash in the mornings, under one of these taps, if you can squeeze a trickle out of one!' Thornton indicated a row of taps over a stone channel where constant dripping had left a deposit of thick green slime. 'You'd better jump out of bed as soon as the bell goes and run for it. There's always a fight for the taps.'

Charles thought of the pretty rose-patterned ewer and basin in his room at the Temple and shuddered, but Thornton was already turning back. 'Come on, dreamy! We don't have to wash now, thank goodness!'

The new boy followed his guide to the sleeping ward over the east side of the cloisters where the younger boys were reluctantly making their way.

The dormitory was lofty with rows of neat beds that looked like shallow wooden trays on iron legs, and there was a settle at the end of each one. Thornton pointed to a bed about halfway down the long room.

'That's yours, and you have to keep it tidy. It's supposed to be a day room as well but woe betide you if you're caught up here in the day without the nurse knowing!'

The freshly sanded floor scrunched under their heavy shoes and the boys began to tiptoe as if they were afraid of disturbing it.

'Hop into bed quickly and don't talk, or the monitor will beat you!' Thornton warned.

Charles hastily obeyed but he could not sleep. He lay for hours looking at the big homely chandelier in the middle of the ceiling, weaving all sorts of fancies around it. He wondered which book Mary was reading all by herself, or if she had the heart to read at all now he was not there.

He had worked himself up into a mood of self-pity

when the loud clangour of a bell made him jump up in a fright. Surely it couldn't be time to get up already? In a panic he shook the sleeping boy next to him.

'Wake up, Thornton, it's the bell!'

Thornton started up in surprise. 'What on earth's the matter?'

'The bell – the bell! Can't you hear it?'

'Shut up – you're *mad*!' Thornton hissed in an undertone. 'That's the public bell. It means that strangers have got to clear out by ten. You'll hear it every night, so for goodness' sake get back to bed and stay there, unless you're yearning for a flogging!'

Charles quickly dived back under the bedclothes and lay still and quiet, wondering what would happen next in this strange place.

He must have dropped to sleep for it was six o'clock next morning when the bell again woke him. The voices of boys all around him, grumbling and yawning, reminded him that he was at school and there was no Aunt Hetty to come to him.

He sprang out of bed, feeling the sand harsh and grating to his bare feet, and followed the others out to the cloisters where he waited, shivering, to get a turn at a tap. A few reluctant drips rewarded his efforts and he made a pretence of dabbing his hands and face before hurrying in to prayers and breakfast.

The boys sat down to a quarter of a penny loaf each and beer served in small wooden pails. Charles sipped cautiously. Ugh! It tasted of the leather jack it was poured from! No wonder most of the boys were drinking water!

From breakfast they trooped into school and Charles forgot the discomforts in his eagerness to begin learning.

Christ's Hospital was divided into five schools. They

were known as the mathematical, or navigation, school, the writing school, the drawing school, the reading school and the grammar school. Being able to read and knowing a little Latin Charles was put at once into the Lower Grammar School, which was held in the same large room as the Upper Grammar School. The two were divided only by an imaginary line, but the contrast between them was so startling that the boy wondered if he had been sent into Bedlam by mistake.

The Lower School was in an uproar, with the boys making paper sundials, playing cats' cradles or making peas dance on a tin pipe, while in the Upper School silence reigned as the pale, frightened-looking scholars struggled on with Plato and Xenophon under the stern eye of the headmaster, the Reverend James Boyer.

'Don't take any notice of them,' said a pleasant-looking boy called Tom Middleton on Charles' first morning. 'We do pretty much as we like this end of the room. Old Boyer's a terror for flogging, but he can't touch us!'

Charles stole a look at the short, stout headmaster. His large hands and face with its sharp nose and mouth and close set eyes looked cruel. He wore a powdered wig and black clerical clothes, with the sleeves short and tight, as if ready to inflict instant punishment. The boy was thankful to be out of range of those big powerful hands and felt sorry for the pupils who felt the weight of them.

'Those big boys spouting Greek are the Grecians – the head boys – the others are Deputy Grecians. Boyer's coaching them for the University – if he doesn't kill them first!'

Charles glanced at these lordly ones in awe, envying their acquaintance with the classics.

'Who teaches us?' he asked.

'The Reverend Matthew Field. He's easy. So long as you mug up a lesson or two from your grammar book, just in case he asks you, you won't have any trouble from him.' Middleton chuckled. 'We don't see a lot of him. If you've come here to swot you'd better try teaching yourself!'

Later on in the day Charles saw his master for the first time, when a tall, dandified figure in clerical clothes came among them. He looked at the boys in his charge as if he wondered why they were there, and began to walk up and down languidly, pausing now and again to ask a question but seldom listening to the answer.

'That's Field!' Middleton nudged Charles.

The master looked at him. 'What did you say, boy?'

'I said "That's Field", sir,' Middleton answered boldly.

'Indeed? And who is he?' Field drawled and sauntered on amid the tittering of the class.

The régime at Christ's Hospital was a Spartan one, but word got round that Charles Lamb was under the patronage of Mr Samuel Salt of the Inner Temple as well as being a friend of Mr Randal Norris, the Sub-Treasurer, and the boy was treated with leniency.

'You're lucky,' Coleridge remarked a trifle bitterly. 'Your Mr Salt's like a screen between you and trouble. Not even the monitors dare take it out of *you*! Every night this week they woke up all the younger boys in our ward and beat us with a strap!'

'W-why?'

'Because someone else had been talking – that's why! That's the kind of justice *we* get!'

Charles wished passionately that he had been beaten rather than have these unfair advantages over his friend.

It was even worse over the matter of food, for Aunt

Hetty very soon discovered that the school meals were both bad and insufficient and decided that *she* would feed her nephew!

Every day she walked from the Temple to Christ's Hospital and waited for the boy to appear. Sometimes he came upon her in the cloisters, sometimes she would be sitting on the coal-hole steps, nursing a basin full of food in her apron.

She would bring it out triumphantly. 'Now eat it all up! They shan't starve you while I'm here!'

It might be a plate of hot veal, or a tasty piece of bacon cooked in his father's kitchen – whatever it was the hungry boy could not resist it and his aunt waited while he cleared up every morsel.

He enjoyed it until he chanced to see Coleridge watching him one day, his eyes dark with longing.

Charles felt a stab of conscience and leapt to his feet calling, 'Col!'

But his friend quickly turned his back and disappeared into the old Grammar School without answering.

Charles was overcome with shame and turned on Aunt Hetty.

'Now look what you've done!' he stuttered angrily and ran after Coleridge.

He found him in the Hall-Play, moodily kicking a ball about.

'Col! I – I'm sorry. I wanted you to share in what my Aunt brought!' the boy stammered.

Coleridge gave the ball an extra hard kick so that it bounced against the wall with a tremendous thud.

'What are you sorry about? I wouldn't eat your precious tit-bits if I were *starving*! You and your hot rolls and tea in the morning – your extra lumps of sugar and ginger –'

thud went the ball again, 'you spoilt kids don't know what it is to live on the school muck!'

'B-but I don't *want* to be treated any better than you, Col! I want to share!' Charles was nearly in tears, 'you — you can have it all next time.'

'Oh, don't talk rot!' Coleridge growled, half ashamed, and walked off with hunched shoulders, leaving the ball to be seized by four juniors of the Writing School.

Charles stamped his foot in a sudden rage. 'It's Aunt Hetty's fault! I won't look for her any more!'

But next morning the pangs of hunger again drove him out to the cloisters where he found the faithful old lady sitting patiently on the steps.

'Come along now, eat up!' she eyed him shrewdly as she undid her apron. 'And don't look so put about. I can't feed six hundred, but I can keep *you* from starving, or my name's not Sarah Lamb!'

The savoury smells coming from the basin were too tempting and the boy gave in. He ate ravenously, trying to keep out of sight of his friends, but his feelings were in a turmoil. He loved Aunt Hetty and wished he didn't feel ashamed of her odd appearances. He felt sorry for the boys who went hungry, but most of all, he wanted to keep Coleridge's friendship.

But hunger won every time and Charles was miserable because he could not conquer it.

He had persuaded himself that his friend would never speak to him again and could hardly believe it when Coleridge came up to him during the dinner break as if nothing had happened.

'We get a whole day leave to-morrow, Charley. Most of the boys go for a swim in the New River, but I don't want to swim. What shall we do?'

'We?' Charles was in the seventh heaven. Col had said we! 'I – I'd like to see the lions in the Tower, Col please.'

Coleridge looked at his small friend with some amusement.

'You love the Royal Menagerie, don't you? All right, we might as well take advantage of our privilege of getting in for nothing. We can look at the book shops on the way.'

The two boys, each wearing a small oval medal in their buttonhole as their badge of leave, set off early in the morning, but they spent so much time with their noses pressed against the glass of the print shops that it was nearly midday when they got to the Tower and they were hungry. They threw themselves down on the grass outside the Lion Tower and Charles shyly produced two meat pies and handed one to his friend.

'Time for dinner, Col,' he said with such a winning smile that Coleridge capitulated.

'You're a cunning little beggar, Charley,' he said gruffly, 'but thanks all the same.'

Charles sighed with relief. Everything was going to be all right.

The days passed happily enough and the gentle, amiable boy became well liked. He had the comfortable feeling that he was only ten minutes walk away from home, and every opportunity he had during that first term he went back to the Temple. Sometimes he took a friend with him, but more often he went alone to satisfy the longing he felt for the dear familiar places.

As Christmas drew near he confided in Aunt Hetty about the festivities the boys at school were preparing.

'We all save up to have a big feast round the fire the night before the holidays. The boys who have a lot share with the ones who haven't anything.' He looked to see if his aunt had taken the hint.

'I'll bring you some extra special goodies,' she promised. 'No one shall say Sarah Lamb's nephew doesn't give *his* share!' She hitched up her apron a trifle belligerently.

There was a breathless sense of excitement in the school as the feast approached. Even the poorest and most friendless boys were caught up in the festive spirit.

On the great day the fire was piled high with logs for once and crackled merrily as the younger boys sat round it in a ring, laughing and joking as they threw chestnuts on the hearth to bake. Now and again someone would burst into a lively carol and the big room would be full of boys' treble voices.

In the light of the leaping flames Charles picked out the faces of many of his new-found friends and returned their smiles. There was George Richards, waving aloft a mince pie, Lancelot Stevens, John Gutch and Tom Middleton, sharing a bag of apples. Edward Thornton and James White, who threw him an orange to catch – Charles knew them all. James White shared his passion for Shakespeare and called out an apt quotation.

'Enjoying it, Charley?' Coleridge dropped down beside the boy and reached for a hot chestnut, throwing it from one hand to the other to cool it.

'Oh, yes! It's like the feast of Lucullus!'

'Or the Inferno! To-morrow we have bread and water again!'

'No – we go home for Christmas to-morrow,' Charles reminded him.

'Not home for me – it's too far. Just friends of my father's – if they remember,' Coleridge finished under his breath as he stared at the flames.

At seven o'clock the younger boys were sent to bed, and Charles lay for a long time looking out at the frosty starlight, listening to the older boys singing carols. It was all strangely beautiful and the imaginative boy saw in his mind's eye the scene on a bleak hillside outside Bethlehem, with the angels singing their song of glory to a handful of frightened men.

Christmas at home was specially happy that year. Mary, grown older and still quieter, could hardly bear to take her eyes from her younger brother, and longed for his usual sweet confidences.

The festivities in the Temple household followed a set, rigid pattern. On Christmas night Mr and Mrs Randal Norris always came over from their rooms in Paper Buildings and Mrs Lamb prided herself on the genteel entertainment she provided for her guests.

Mr Norris beamed at the sight of Charles, standing proud and self-conscious in his bluecoat uniform.

'Ah, my boy, how's the world of learning? *Labor omnia vincit,* eh?' The chance to air his small knowledge of Latin pleased the Sub-Treasurer. 'I take it you're learning Latin?'

'Oh, yes, sir,' the boy replied eagerly, 'I like it!'

'Good! Splendid! There's nothing like *knowledge,* Charley.'

'And there's nothing like a good, rollicking song on Christmas night, Randal,' John Lamb put in heartily. 'Let's hear from you.'

For all the world as if he had a large repertoire Mr Norris hesitated, then said, 'Er – yes. How about this one?' before he proceeded to sing the only song he knew.

Charles had heard it ever since he could remember Christmas but he still looked forward to it as an established custom. It alluded to a threatened invasion, but he was not quite sure which one.

Mr Norris threw back his head and his eyes sparkled with excitement when he came to the passage

> We still make 'em run and we'll still make 'em sweat,
> In spite of the devil and *Brussels Gazette*!

Everyone clapped and called 'Bravo!' as the singer sat down, mopping his forehead and trying to look modest.

Sometimes brother John could be prevailed upon to sing a ballad in his weak tenor and Mr Lamb never needed much prompting to recite some of his own doggerel, while the womenfolk would bustle about making sure there was plenty to eat and drink.

It all passed too quickly and the grown-up world of work and cares again ousted the magic.

Christ's Hospital had fifteen days' holiday at Christmas and Charles still had another week at home. He spent most of it looking for new books in Mr Salt's library, which was always open to him.

'What are you so taken up with?' Mary asked fretfully when she discovered him with half a dozen books around him.

'Latin,' said her brother grandly. 'I can read it quite well now. Listen!' And he read a few passages from Ovid with ease and fluency.

'Oh, *that*!' Mary said disparagingly. 'You're getting to be quite conceited, Charley. You scarcely look at an English book these days. We used to read Shakespeare together and you always found the prettiest places for me.' She turned aside in disappointment. 'I suppose I shall have to puzzle it out alone now.'

'No, Mary!' Her brother jumped up quickly. 'We'll read Shakespeare again, and I'll teach you Latin as well. Then we can go on reading everything together!'

Mary nodded dubiously. 'I'll try hard to learn, Charley, but I still like Shakespeare best of all.'

6

Deputy Grecian

As his schooldays progressed Charles Lamb made many friends. Most of them were his senior by at least two years, but because he was their intellectual equal no one took account of his age.

It was proof of the general feeling of kindliness towards him that no one laughed at him or mimicked his incurable stammer. Even the tough 'Mathemats' of the Naval School – the King's Boys – found no fun in ridiculing a boy who gave nothing but a gentle, dreamy smile in return.

He loved to write verse, pouring out his secret thoughts in high-sounding words and phrases. Half shyly, he showed his first efforts to Coleridge.

'These are *good,* Charley,' Coleridge pronounced after long study. 'I don't think I did half so well at your age.'

The boy flushed with pleasure. 'But *your* poems are wonderful, Col! They make me feel as if I'm being lifted up to the skies!'

'Thanks. But then I'm nearly three years older than you,' Coleridge felt bound to put on a superior tone. 'You're doing very well.'

It was a Sunday and the boys were walking home from Christ Church in Newgate Street, where long morning and afternoon services took the place of weekday school time.

They were a familiar pair, the one big and thick-set, the other small and fragile, with a slow, plodding walk that made him look oddly staid and elderly. Out of school they were inseparable.

Charles folded his poems and tucked them away carefully in an inner pocket as they strolled across the Hall playground.

'I wish it were not Sunday,' he said. 'I don't like these awful public suppers, with crowds coming to stare at us. It makes me feel as if I'm in the Royal Menagerie!'

'We're stared at in Church nearly as much,' Coleridge said reasonably. 'We must look a sight – six hundred of us looking as if we're suspended in the air each side of the organ! Charity children, that's what we are, and the wealthy people like to look at us and tell themselves how good they are to support us in such *luxury*!' His tone was sarcastic. 'That's the object of the public suppers, anyway.'

'Mr Salt told me they're to *interest* the public. That's a different thing,' Charles argued.

'Then it's confoundedly difficult to distinguish between genuine interest and downright vulgar curiosity,' Coleridge summed it up shrewdly. 'But there's the bell. Let's go in and start the show.'

They made for the Hall and stood behind their seats at the long tables. Soon the stately procession entered, led by a beadle carrying a two hundred year old mace and followed closely by the Treasurer and other dignitaries. The usual time-honoured prayers were said before the formal 'bowing round' of the boys.

There was a touch of medieval pageantry about the whole ceremony, with the beadle wearing robes of a pattern as old as the mace itself and the great company of boys in their traditional Tudor uniform in the splendour of the well-lighted Hall.

'You'd think we were going to have a Lord Mayor's banquet instead of a miserable bit of bread and cheese,' muttered John Gutch resentfully.

These weekly public suppers made all the boys feel uncomfortable and were an ordeal for Charles, who hated being stared at. It seemed to him that all the well-dressed citizens of London came to look round with blatant curiosity, asking idiotic questions of the embarrassed boys.

'I don't know why they all look so self-satisfied,' he grumbled afterwards.

'We flatter the universal instinct for the antique,' Valentine le Grice explained humourously. 'Look at these noble walls! Everything's at least two hundred years old, and by the look of the beadle's clothes, I swear they're the original ones!'

Charles chuckled appreciatively. Next to Coleridge, le Grice was his greatest friend.

'My Godfather Fielde should recommend us to Sheridan! We'd look fine at Garrick's Drury – all glitter and no grub!'

'You're getting cynical, Charles Lamb!'

The older boys moved into the common rooms as the younger ones dispersed to bed. This was a free time when friends gathered together in small groups, to talk about the things that interested them most. Charles was always the centre of the most intellectual group.

'It'll soon be Easter, Charley, then you'll have to put up with more pomp and ceremony,' Val le Grice teased him gently.

'Oh, I don't mind the Easter procession. It's one of the traditions I like,' Charles answered with a smile. 'Besides we get eleven days' holiday at the end of it.'

'But first we have to endure the Spital sermons. They might be good if anyone ever *heard* them, but all we hear is a rumbling in the valley, with the preacher's head moving up and down like a chicken pecking up corn!' The boys laughed. 'I must say this for my Pater,' le Grice went on, 'he *thunders* out his sermons so that the whole village can hear!'

'I can't remember the last time I heard mine preach,' Coleridge joined in glumly. 'I believe I'd even bear one of his pi-jaws for the sake of a sight of home!'

'Cheer up!' le Grice slapped him on the back heartily, 'you shall have two solid hours of old Sandiford on Easter Tuesday.'

Coleridge groaned. 'The only thing that keeps me going is the thought of the Lord Mayor's buns beforehand!'

'And his sixpence!' Charles cried. 'Remember our first

sixpences, Col, and the books we bought with them?'

His mind went back to his first Easter at the school. How thrilled he had been to be one of that great procession of Bluecoat boys marching through the City streets to the Mansion House! He thought of the new gloves he had been given with a paper on them which read 'He is Risen' which he was told to pin on his left breast. Then the boys had moved off, proud as an army with banners – the Mathemats with their distinctive silver badges gleaming on their shoulders, carrying a ruler and compass, the Writing School boys with a red pen in their ears, the Reading School carrying Bibles or Testaments and the Grammar School with their traditional grammar books. Half the City turned out to see them and cheer them on.

The small boy had secretly hero-worshipped the tall, dignified Grecians who led the procession as if they were a royal cavalcade, straight to the place where the Lord Mayor and his Aldermen were waiting to distribute the customary gifts of buns and wine, chatting and joking to the boys meanwhile.

Charles never forgot the mixture of panic and pleasure he felt when a stout, hearty alderman spoke to him.

'Grammar School boy, eh? How d'you like it, boy?'

The boy had managed to stutter out that he liked it very well.

'That's what I like to hear! Wouldn't do to waste public money on you, y'know. And I wager you've set your sights on the University, heh?'

'I – I mean to try, sir,' the eight year old boy had responded bravely.

'Good lad! We'll see you get there!' the alderman promised grandly and moved on to talk with another boy.

The University! Charles had felt the first surge of

ambition. He'd heard the masters and the Grecians talk of
this Paradise of learning. He *must* get there! It was like a
sudden vision of a Promised Land.

In a dream, he had been pushed on to receive his sixpence. The Grecians had half a guinea and the monitors
a shilling each, but that sixpence was like a fortune to
Charles.

Thornton had whispered to him during the long sermon
which followed, 'What are you going to buy?'

'Books.' The reply came without hesitation.

'You *are* a swot, Charles Lamb!' Thornton was dis-
gusted. 'I'm going to buy buns – as many as I can get!'

Now, six years later, Coleridge recalled laughingly how
they had rushed out to Paternoster Row and exasperated
all the booksellers in their frantic search for bargains.

'I bought a Virgil. I've nearly worn it out since.'

'I bought my first book of Spenser,' Charles sighed. 'I
shall never part with it.'

'You're an incurable sentimentalist, Charley,' le Grice
said. 'You'll soon have the finest library of shabby second-
hand first-rate books in the kingdom!'

Charles joined in the laughter at his expense.

'It doesn't matter how shabby books are – it's what's
between the covers that counts!'

Charles and Coleridge had never failed to spend their
Easter bounty on books. First choice were the classics and
Coleridge became so enthralled with the sagas of ancient
Greece and Rome that he was often to be seen walking up
and down the playground, reciting from Homer or Pindar
in the original Greek, with Charles his willing and admiring audience. His deep, sweet intonation made many a
passer-by pause to listen in amazement.

'That charity boy is inspired!' said an elderly cleric to

his companion. 'Just listen to him reciting the Odyssey!'

Tom Middleton, now a deputy Grecian, paused to listen one day and asked curiously, 'Is that a task?'

Coleridge looked over his book with a gleam of humour in his luminous eyes.

'No, Middleton, it's a pleasure.'

Afterwards he confided in Charles, 'I wish I hadn't been so clever. Middleton told old Boyer what I said and now he is taking an "interest" in me. You know what *that* means! Extra grinding – and extra floggings!'

'But you don't need to grind, Col. I've never heard anyone so good at reciting Latin and Greek! Have you made up any more verses?'

'Lots. They just seem to seethe around in my brain and tumble out. Sometimes I can't get any peace until I've written them down! Do you feel like that too, Charley?'

'Yes,' Charles confessed slowly, 'but I like to write about what I see – people and places. Sometimes I think I like places more than people.'

The two were walking down Fleet Street, on their way to the Temple to spend a precious half holiday's freedom in some of Charles' favourite haunts.

'I expect old Boyer's got his eye on you for a Grecian, Col,' the boy went on as they made their way to the fountain in Hare Court to quench their thirst.

Coleridge looked round in alarm. 'You don't really think so?'

'Why not? He knows you're certain to get through to the University.'

'I don't mind the University. In fact, I want that more than anything.'

'Then you'll have to be a Grecian first! It's the law of the Medes and Persians, isn't it?'

They had reached the fountain and Coleridge pressed the button so hard that a cascade of water shot out and drenched him. He shook his head slowly and the drops of water fell from his glossy black hair in a shower.

'I don't want to be a Grecian!' he said emphatically. 'I don't care for all the idiotic rules and regulations that go with it! All the Grecians have got to make public speeches – all Grecians have got to enter the Church – ! No, thank you, I'm determined not to do that.'

'Why not?' Charles argued, 'Sam le Grice is taking Orders, isn't he?'

The boys cupped their hands and drank deeply of the sparkling cold water before Coleridge replied.

'Sam's different. He's cut out for it, I'm not. I want a wider life than that, Charley. I want to be free to write and I don't want to be told what I've got to write about.'

But his protests were in vain. The Reverend James Boyer recognized genius when he saw it and selected Coleridge for a Grecianship. From then on 'That sensible fool, Coleridge', as he was heard to call him, alternately delighted and bewildered his tyrannical master.

When Charles was promoted to the Upper School he too came under the dreaded Mr Boyer, who, however, was careful to keep his hands off Mr Salt's protégé.

It was not long before the boy was made a deputy Grecian, a rank second only in importance to the lordly Grecians. Now he read Homer and Horace, Demosthenes and Cicero, and revelled in the books of his dreams.

The Latin and English verses he made in class were of such high standard that they won Boyer's grudging praise.

'You may read them to us, Charles Lamb,' he said magnanimously one afternoon, waving aside the exercise the boy held out to him.

Crimson-faced, Charles stood up and tried to recite his own lines, but the words would not come. His face contorted with the effort and the sound, when it came at all, was an unintelligible stutter. The class was silent and sympathetic. No one looked at the embarrassed boy.

'Sit down, child, and don't ruin the verses you've written,' the irate master roared. 'Pass 'em up!' He held out his big hand peremptorily.

Charles felt frustrated and despondent as he watched his poem under that cold sardonic gaze. What would the master say? Would he tear it up in contempt?

'H'm,' said Boyer at length and turned his fishy stare on his nervous pupil. 'You shall write that in my manuscript book, boy.'

'Oh, s-sir!' Charles gasped incredulously, 'd-does that mean – ?'

'It means that it's of more than ordinary merit, or I should not allow it to appear in my book. Don't gibber, child!'

It was such a signal honour that the boy could hardly believe it. The headmaster's book contained many exercises penned by old boys who were already famous. The school was proud of it – it was a coveted distinction to appear in it.

When school had finished for the day Charles went to collect the manuscript book.

'Write it in a fair hand, Charles Lamb, or odd's my life, I'll flog you!'

Since all Boyer's commands were accompanied by a threat the boy took very little notice. He was far too engrossed in the precious book.

Left to himself he turned back the pages and saw inscribed *Julia*, by Samuel Taylor Coleridge. A page or two later this was followed by *The Progress of Vice, Monody on Chatterton* and *Quae Nocent Docent* – all signed with Coleridge's familiar signature. Charles' heart swelled with pride in his friend.

With fast beating heart he turned to a clean page and stared at it for a moment or two while he tried to control the trembling of his hands. He was not a tidy writer – he had to be careful. He penned the title of his poem slowly and painstakingly:

Mille Viae Mortis

There was no sound but the heavy ticking of the big clock on the wall as the pendulum swung the minutes into the lost limbo of the day. Soon the scratching of the boy's pen joined it in an odd kind of duet, a macabre accompaniment to his thoughts on death.

> What time in bands of slumber all were laid
> To Death's dark court, methought I was convey'd,
> In realms it lay far hid from mortal sight,
> And gloomy tapers scarce kept out the night.
>
> On ebon throne the King of Terrors sate,
> Around him stood the ministers of Fate;
> On fell destruction bent, the murth'rous band
> Waited attentively his high command.
>
> Here pallid Fear and dark Despair were seen,
> And Fever here with looks forever lean,
> Swoln Dropsy, halting Gout, profuse of woes,
> And Madness fierce and hopeless of repose.
>
> Wide-wasting Plague; but chief in honour stood
> More-wasting War, insatiable of blood;
> With starting eye-balls, eager for the word:
> Already brandish'd was the glittering sword.

Wonder and fear alike had fill'd my breast,
And thus the grisly Monarch I addrest –
'Of earth-born Heroes why should poets sing,
And thee neglect, neglect the greatest King?
To thee ev'n Caesar's self was forc'd to yield
The glories of Pharsalia's well-fought field.'

When with a frown, 'Vile caitiff, come not here!'
Abrupt cried Death; 'Shall flatt'ry soothe my ear?'
'Hence, or thou feel'st my dart!' the Monarch said.
Wild terror seiz'd me, and the vision fled.'

It was done! With a sigh of satisfaction the boy added his signature, 'Charles Lamb', and waited for the ink to dry on his first recorded poem.

He put the book away and stole out to the cloisters to be alone under the stars – to think. He had written his poem, it is true, but he'd made an ass of himself in class.

It was always the same. If he tried to speak about the things he felt most deeply his vocal cords contracted, his jaws stiffened and no sound came but unintelligible gibberish. He might as well be an ape! he thought disgustedly. Week after week he listened enviously to the Grecians practising the art of speech-making in class. Why could he not do the same? He felt as if an evil spirit possessed him and he felt afraid.

The mood of self-pity passed and he went to the Grecians' Common Room to find Coleridge.

He found that youth passionately declaiming in Latin prose the merits of the Royal Hospitals, the other Grecians listening in mock boredom.

'This was the noblest of them all!' quoted le Grice, his blue eyes twinkling at Charles.

Bob Allen's ready laugh rang out and echoed round the lofty room.

'Bravo, Charley! You do us honour!' His fair, handsome face was wreathed in smiles.

Favell looked up from the depths of an armchair. His long legs sprawled before him showing a length of bright yellow stocking.

'For goodness sake, stop Col spouting, Charles Lamb! He's been at it this past hour!'

Coleridge paused. 'Shut up, Favell! You know I've got to do the Latin oration on Speech Day. I've got to get myself in trim.'

'Well, you *are* in trim, and all set to blast the governors out of their seats, I should say. I bet they won't understand a word you're talking about, anyway. Why not tell them a few home truths?'

'Are you really delivering the oration, Col?' Charles could not conceal his admiration.

'Yes, for my sins, I am.' Coleridge pretended to be reluctant but his friends knew that he liked nothing better than speaking in Latin. He was already a complete master of rhetoric.

Speech Day at Christ's Hospital coincided with St Matthew's Day and proceedings began with a service in Christ Church.

It was a mellow September day and the trees in the churchyard rustled their gold-tinged leaves in anticipation of autumn as the boys trooped back to the Great Hall to listen to two of their number, chosen from the élite of the school, deliver their own original speeches before the governors.

Charles watched Coleridge as he mounted the steps to the pulpit, proud as a young god. With an imperious gesture he brushed the thick black hair from his brow and faced the governors, supremely confident of his own

D

powers. With a superb touch he spoke of some of the great men of the past who had done honour to the school by being educated in it, and the boy's sweet voice and impassioned delivery moved many of his hearers to wipe away a furtive tear, whether they understood him or not.

Charles suspected that Coleridge was not even conscious of his audience until the applause greeted the end of his oration.

The next Grecian spoke in English verse, a masterly performance that caused Mr Boyer to turn to the governors with a superior smile as if to say, '*My* coaching did that! I made these boys into scholars that have no equal in the land!'

While the applause lasted the boys shared in that pride, the hardships and suffering forgotten for a fleeting moment. To-morrow the bread and water régime would begin again, the harsh discipline and the cruel bullying take up relentless sway.

The year was 1789 and it was destined to be Charles Lamb's last Speech Day. Two months later he was told that he would have to leave Christ's Hospital.

'It's b-because of my beastly stuttering!' he told Coleridge miserably. 'I can't make a speech, so I can't be a Grecian. There's no place for me here.'

'It's a wretched shame, Charley. You ought to have gone on to the University.'

'I haven't a hope now,' Charles said sadly.

He said good-bye to his friends with a lump in his throat, then took off his blue gown for the last time and exchanged it for a coat and neckcloth.

He shook hands solemnly with the astonished beadle as he passed through the great gate into Newgate Street, no longer a schoolboy.

He looked back at the ancient building that had been his Alma Mater – the splendid Hall with the towers at each end, where he had so often listened to the strains of the organ and the choir; the cloisters where the monks used to walk and the schools grouped round the great playgrounds – these were the places he loved and would never forget.

'I'll come back,' he vowed, 'I'll come as often as I can.'

Then with slow plodding steps he walked towards the Temple and home.

He mustered up a smile as Mary greeted him with affection.

'Oh, Charley! I'm so glad you're home! Don't go away any more, will you?'

He tried to shake off the strange feeling of loss and emptiness that gripped him.

'We'll have time to go to some plays now, Mary!' he said brightly. 'I'm looking forward to that.'

His mother sniffed disparagingly.

'Plays, indeed! It's high time you thought of work, Charley. Goodness knows, we need another wage coming in this house, with your father getting more and more irresponsible – '

7

The Meeting with Elia

In spite of the difference in their ages Mary looked to her
fifteen-year-old brother as she would to an equal.

'Charley, you are the one person in all this world I can
turn to,' she said in despair. 'Sometimes I feel as if I'm
lost in the dark – and evil hands are waiting to pull me
down into a deep pit!' She shuddered, covering her face
with her hands. 'It *frightens* me so! Suppose I should not

be able to get out? I couldn't *live* there, Charley!'

'You wouldn't have to live there, Mary. I'd get you out.' Her brother reminded her quietly. 'You know I'll always help you.'

Reassured, Mary gave him a winning smile, so like his own, then turned to her sewing again.

'Father's getting very feeble. Hadn't you noticed?'

'Yes, I had noticed.' Charles sat at the table, idly turning the leaves of a book, but his mind was troubled. 'What's the matter with him? He can't concentrate or write verse like he used to – his mind's in a perpetual muddle.'

Mary sighed. 'We're all getting older, Charley. Father's just getting a little bit childish, as some elderly people do.'

'Perhaps that's what it is,' the boy studied his sister's face anxiously. He realized with a shock that she was a grown woman now. Twenty-five! It seemed a great age to him. 'I wish John hadn't left home,' he went on. 'Mother must miss him so much.'

'Oh, she does,' Mary snipped off an end of thread. 'She always liked John best, didn't she? But of course he's twenty-six now and wanted a place of his own.'

'I don't see why. He could have stayed here.'

'But he's got an important position –' Mary hesitated. Her eyes suddenly clouded and she looked at Charles vacantly. 'Where – Charley?'

'He's a clerk at South Sea House,' the boy reminded her gently.

Her pale face cleared and she smiled again. 'That's it. The last time he came to see us he told us all about the grand lodgings he has and the collection of paintings he's getting together. He's so *handsome* – Mother's so proud of him!'

Charles got up impatiently and stared down into the fire moodily.

'A clerk! I don't envy him his dull, monotonous grind! I want to write, Mary! I want to write poems and prose that people will remember to eternity! Do you know what I wrote in Mr Boyer's book?'

Mary shook her head.

'Then listen!'

With his back to the fireplace and his spindly legs planted firmly apart Charles began to recite *Mille Viae Mortis.*

Mary watched the changing expressions on his fine, intelligent face and tears of tenderness came into her eyes.

– 'And Madness fierce and hopeless of repose – '

Mrs Lamb walked into the room in time to hear these words. She stopped short, an expression of aversion on her face.

'That's enough talk of madness in *this* house, my boy,' she said, coldly angry.

'It's – it's only a poem, Mother,' her son began to stammer, 'the one I wrote at school.'

'Then it's a pity they didn't teach you something more useful. All these idle fancies will get you nowhere.'

With a gesture of resignation Charles stalked out of the room. He caught a glimpse of Aunt Hetty through the doorway of her room, muttering her devotions with the fevered air of a fanatic. She was more gaunt than ever, with deep lines etched round her eyes and mouth – lines of bitterness and sorrow. The boy felt the tense atmosphere closing round him like a trap and hurried out to take refuge in Mr Salt's library.

Two days later Mr Coventry sent for him and Charles learned that once again he had to thank his patrons of the

Inner Temple for 'a start in life', as his father put it.

'H'm – *ha-a-a*!' A cloud of snuff temporarily eclipsed the big square face of the eminent lawyer and the boy looked at him through a haze. 'My friend, Joseph Paice, is willing to give you the run of his counting house, boy, until something better turns up,' Mr Coventry boomed out. 'Mind you make the most of it. You'll learn business routine – good for you!' He dived beneath his coat flaps for more snuff.

Charles could only stammer out a miserable, 'Thank you, s-sir!'

'Paice is a merchant in Bread Street Hill. Present yourself at his office next Monday at nine of the morning – sharp!' Coventry inhaled deeply and dismissed the boy.

His father looked anxious as they walked across the Court homewards.

'It's a grand chance, son. Aren't you pleased?'

The disappointed boy was about to make a bitter comment when he caught sight of his father's face puckered with anxiety. There was a baffled and bewildered look in his eyes, as if he could no longer cope with the problems of a family.

'Y-yes, Father, I'm pleased,' Charles knew the sacrifice was expected of him and he faced it dutifully.

Mrs Lamb was openly jubilant. 'Now perhaps you'll forget all this nonsense about poetry. You'll have to curb your imagination in an office, my boy!'

'Poor Charley!' Mary whispered gently.

Rather reluctantly, Charles made his way to Bread Street Hill the following Monday morning.

An anæmic looking clerk seated on a high stool in the outer office did not bother to unwind his legs and descend from his perch.

'I want to see Mr Paice,' Charles began nervously.

'What for?' the clerk adjusted his paper cuffs carefully.

'Work. Mr Coventry of the Inner Temple sent me.'

The clerk looked down his nose. 'My! Some people have grand friends, haven't they?' He jerked a thumb over his shoulder indicating a panelled mahogany door at the back. 'In there, youngster! That's the guv'nor's den.'

Mr Paice was not the ogre that Charles had imagined. In fact, he was a genial, courteous gentleman whose kindly manner soon put the nervous boy at his ease.

'So you're Charles Lamb. My friend Coventry told me about you. An old Blue, I believe?'

'Y-yes, sir.' The boy warmed to the kindly tones.

'I hope you'll like it here. It's just a temporary post, you know, so that you can learn a little about commerce. You're a bright boy, I'm told. No doubt you'll take to it quickly.'

But Charles did not take to business life very readily. It was only because of his great liking for Mr Paice, who seemed to be a modern Sir Galahad, that he tried to master the various ledgers.

'They're cold, dead books,' he said to a fellow clerk in disgust.

The man looked at him in astonishment. 'You're crazy – that's what's the matter with you!'

Whatever he did, Charles found that ideas for essays or lines of poems would keep coming between him and the figures he was trying to work on. He began to keep a notebook, jotting down these odd thoughts when he could and showing them to Mary in the evening.

Now and again he met Coleridge in the City and they would haunt the book shops together. At one of these chance meetings he found his friend turning the pages of a small book with a look of reverence on his face.

'Look at this, Charley! I've discovered something that's done my heart more good than all the other books I've ever read, except the Bible.'

Charles took the slim volume held out to him.

'William Lisle Bowles,' he read from the title page.'

'Yes. It's his first book. There are fourteen sonnets – so tender and sad that they wring the heart out of you! They're great, Charley – absolutely great!'

Charles was already reading the poems eagerly, his eyes deeply thoughtful. The poet's soft strains suited his melancholy mood.

'They're beautiful, Col – almost like Virgil, but they're modern. Bowles puts into words what we're thinking. The older folk will think he's too advanced.'

The friends discussed the new poet excitedly as they paced the City streets, oblivious of the jostling crowds and the hucksters crying their wares.

'I'm going up to Cambridge soon, to Jesus College,' Coleridge announced suddenly.

Charles suppressed a pang of envy. 'I'm glad for you, Col, but I shall miss you.'

'I can come to London occasionally. We'll meet at the old tavern by Smithfield – "The Salutation and Cat". Remember it?'

They smiled as they thought of the illicit visits during school days.

'It'll be something to look forward to. I'll save up all my high-falutin' literary conversation for you, Col. You'll have to listen to all my effusions – if I have time or heart to write any!'

'You will,' said Coleridge confidently. 'You're a born scribbler, Charley.'

Not long after this conversation Mr Paice sent for Charles.

'Well, my boy, you've learned a little here, I hope, and now I can offer you a clerkship in the South Sea Company. Your brother John has spoken for you.'

'Oh – I didn't know – ' Charles mumbled, surprised.

Mr Paice beamed. 'I am a director and Mr Coventry is a governor of the Company, so you have a threefold recommendation.'

'Thank you, sir,' the boy replied automatically.

'It's a splendid opening, and you will receive a salary of ten and six a week – far more than I had when I was a boy!'

The benevolent gentleman sat back in his chair and regarded his young employee with satisfaction.

'I know you will do us credit, Lamb.'

Charles tried to summon up a little enthusiasm for his new post as he walked home that night. Another office – more dusty ledgers and day books and files! What was the use of a classical education?

'I feel like Andromeda chained to a rock,' he muttered to himself, 'only my rock's a desk.'

He was not expected at South Sea House immediately and he was a little cheered when his mother suggested a visit to his grandmother to take her news of the family.

He was saddened to find the old lady very much aged.

Ben told him, 'She's ill, Master Charley, mortal ill!'

'I wonder anyone can be so brave!' the boy exclaimed.

'Ah, she's brave right enough, and patient. She never grouses nor grumbles like most sick folks do.'

'Perhaps that's because she's a Christian, Ben. A *real* Christian, I mean, not just a Sunday one.'

Charles sat and talked to his grandmother until at

length she began to get weary and sent him out to get some fresh air. He was only too pleased to walk in the quiet lanes and get the smoke and grime of London out of his lungs.

It was August and the summer was beginning to wane. The countryside was in full luxuriant growth and the hedges were heavy with the rich scarlet fruit of the dog rose. He was strolling towards Widford, idly cutting at the wayside nettles with a stick when he saw a girl standing pensively by a gate. He paused, struck by her resemblance to the child with a lamb in the picture at Blakesware House.

The girl looked at this small, soberly dressed youth curiously. Her eyelashes fluttered artlessly over light blue eyes and her fair hair glinted in the sun like golden gossamer.

'I beg your pardon. Did you speak to *me*?' she replied to Charles' incoherent stammering.

'No, ma'am, but I ask leave to do so now.'

She lowered her head to hide a smile at his old-fashioned courtesy which, had she known it, was in fair imitation of Mr Paice.

'I wondered if you were a Miss Plumer?' Charles spoke hesitantly. 'You see, in the Plumers' house at Blakesware – where my grandmother lives – there is a portrait which might be you. As a child, I mean – ' He began to flounder.

'Alas, no, I am plain Anne Simmonds and I live at Blenheims.'

Charles bowed gravely. 'Charles Lamb, at your service, Miss Simmonds.'

Their eyes met and they laughed.

'Oh, dear, aren't we dreadfully correct?' Anne's blue eyes danced. 'I'm sure even my papa would approve!'

. They walked together down the country lane towards Blenheims and talked as if they had known each other all their lives. Charles' stammer scarcely plagued him at all as he chatted eagerly with this golden girl of his dreams.

It was the first of many meetings and the lad's infatuation grew. The prospect of returning to the Temple did not please him but he swore to write love sonnets to Anne when they were separated.

By September 1st he was tied to another desk and Blakesware was again far away.

He was just sixteen and a half when he entered the magnificent porticos of South Sea House, a great decaying building near the Bank.

Charles, dressed with Quakerish simplicity in black, was told to report to the Examiners' Office and was directed to an enormous room, peopled by a few straggling clerks making a pretence of working. They looked more like domestic retainers in a great house than business men, thought the bewildered boy.

An old-fashioned, middle-aged clerk was nibbing a pen with an air of profound seriousness as Charles entered. He paused and nodded gravely.

'Master Lamb, if I mistake not? I see little family likeness to Mr John. A jovial handsome fellow, our Mr John.'

A gleam of humour lit up Charles' face.

'Brothers do not necessarily reflect the same image, sir.'

'Eh? No. Pity.' And Mr Hepworth returned to the solemn and absorbing business of nibbing his pen.

Charles approached the cashier who was poring over his books at the counter. He was the most extraordinary looking man he had ever seen, with a very red face and powdered hair frizzed out like a caricature of an old time beau.

'P-please, sir – ' Charles began.

'Evans is the name, boy, Evans! What d'you want?'

'I want to know where to sit – I've come to work here.'

'Odds-my-life, yes! So you have! Here, take this,' he thrust a great ledger into the boy's hands. 'Add up these columns – over there!' He indicated a desk. 'And don't interrupt me when I'm making up my cash or I'll have your skin!' His fingers trembled over his cash boxes and he glared around as if he suspected everyone of being a defaulter.

Charles slipped into an empty place quietly, but he could not focus his attention on the figures before him for looking at the odd assortment of men around him.

A mild, elderly gentleman was softly practising the German flute, a sheet of music on his open ledger page, another was busy completing a pen and ink sketch of his neighbour.

'A mixed bunch – like a Noah's Ark, aren't they?' the man in the desk next to Charles said in a friendly tone.

He was very tall and thin, with a dark, swarthy look about him that was slightly foreign. The hollowness of his jaws emphasised the smouldering fire of his dark eyes, and the thick black hair that grew on his temples gave him an air of distinction.

Charles smiled, pleased to be spoken to. 'Yes – it's different here. If it were not a business house I might like it.'

'Don't you like business either?' the dark man asked.

'No. I – I've no taste for it.'

'But perhaps you have a taste for other things.'

Charles nodded warily.

'Now I – I want to write,' his companion went on dreamily. 'Every evening when I get home to my lodgings I take up my pen – a different kind of pen – ' he gazed at the one in his hand distastefully, 'then I write down my thoughts.' His thin shoulders heaved in a sigh. 'Ah, well, I don't suppose I'll ever do more than that. Authorship doesn't feed a man, does it?'

'That's what everyone tells *me*!' On a sudden impulse Charles added, 'All the same, I'd rather be a poet than the richest merchant in the City of London!'

'So – ! I've found a kindred spirit at last – Charles Lamb!' The clerk reached out a long arm and shook Charles' hand warmly, rather to that youth's embarrassment.

'Thanks. What's your name?'

'Elia – just call me that.'

'Elia!' Charles repeated it softly. 'It has a musical ring to it. It's a good name – easy to remember.'

Elia was pleased with his young friend's fancy.

'It is Italian. I was born in the land of the sun!' With a sudden change of mood he sighed. 'I don't suppose anyone will ever hear of it again when I die.'

'Who knows?' Charles joked, 'You may be famous!'

The Italian clerk's friendship helped Charles to settle down in this new post. His gift of imagination, almost equal to Charles' own, made the old place come alive. He peopled it again with the ghosts of the past until they could almost hear the raucous cries of the merchants and see the desks set up in the streets as the gambling fever of the early part of the century swept through the City like a plague.

Sometimes in the evenings, when the peace and quiet was almost cloistral, the two clerks would wander slowly through the bare rooms and courts of the old house, their footsteps echoing as they passed through the long passages hung with rows of buckets.

'There's enough water here to subdue an inferno!' Elia peered at the contents of the pails. 'Ugh! And enough putrefaction to start another plague!'

They opened a massive mahogany door and found themselves in a huge disused room. In the middle was a long table, once rich mahogany, now worm-eaten, with a tarnished gilt leather covering on which stood great silver ink-stands.

Elia lifted one and examined it curiously. 'Our forebears were rich merchants, Charles, by the look of these things. To think that this forgotten old place was once as important as the Bank or the Exchange!'

Charles was looking at the portraits of pompous governors, with Queen Anne and other monarchs, hung around the walls. He came to a huge chart.

'Look at this, Elia! It might give the clue to hidden treasure!'

'Not likely!' Elia laughed. 'It wouldn't be here for all the clerks to see if it did. It just indicates the places where trade was done in the region of the South Seas. They must have made some discoveries in the Bay of Panama too, by the look of these old soundings!'

They found a map of Mexico, dusty and brittle with age, and Charles vowed he could trace the finger prints where a ghostly hand had pointed the way to the treasures of El Dorado.

But it was the old-time books which fascinated the two clerks most of all. Their curious fingers disturbed layers of dust as they explored the methods of book-keeping in Queen Anne's reign.

'These vellum covers are beautiful!' Charles touched them reverently. 'They ought to be safe in a library.' He turned the pages carefully. 'Look at the way they began all their dealings – commending everything to God!'

'I suppose God wishes to enter into our commercial enterprises. We should not keep Him shut in a church!'

Charles grew deeply thoughtful. 'You're right, Elia. But if people meant what they said in these books there would never have been such a fraud as the South Sea Bubble.'

'Perhaps not. We're all hypocrites at heart. We say one thing and mean another,' Elia spoke sadly.

'It's lying!' Charles answered passionately. 'I mean to stand for the truth, Elia, no matter what happens!'

'And a good thing, my young friend. But you must acknowledge that our forefathers lied with dignity and appreciated beauty.' He picked up a large pounce box and shook out some of the fine powder with which the clerks dried the ink. 'These boxes are better than ours. They give an air of importance to an office. The powder is still quite dry, too. I wonder if some ghostly accountant comes here at night to keep his precious books in order?'

Slowly and surely South Sea House and its curious collection of clerks played its part in influencing the young Charles Lamb's character. His strong individuality developed apace and with it came courage.

His friendship with Elia made up in part for the loss of his friends at Christ's Hospital, most of whom had by now dispersed to universities or entered some profession.

Once again there was change in store. Charles had been in the service of the South Sea Company for five months when the death of Mr Samuel Salt threw his family into a state of confusion.

His father was quite unable to cope with the change that had come upon him, Mrs Lamb was in failing health and Aunt Hetty was now too old to assume responsibility, even if her sister-in-law had tolerated it. It was generally agreed that Mary must not be troubled. The whole family looked to its youngest member to help them.

Charles left his employment and went home to the Temple, the better to sort out his parents' affairs.

8

The Reluctant Clerk

Charles was relieved to learn that Mr Salt had left legacies to his parents. They were little enough, it is true, but it saved them from poverty, for John Lamb had been careless with money and there was nothing put by for 'a rainy day'. The loss of his old employer sent him completely to pieces and it was clear to his son that Mr Lamb was now too feeble and childish to work any more.

Mary's dressmaking brought in a living for herself but the dark threat of insanity hung like a perpetual cloud over her. No one could say when the cloud would descend and make her incapable of work for a time.

The uncertainty of the future was in all their minds and Mary was most anxious for her brother. She sought him out one day as he was taking a last look round Mr Salt's library – soon to be broken up and sold.

'Charley, what are you going to do?'

He knew what she meant. 'I shall have to get another post, Mary, and soon.'

Her eyes grew troubled. 'I wish you need not.'

He smiled cheerfully. 'As a matter of fact, I have been speaking to Mr Peter Pierson. He was a friend of Mr Salt's, you know.' He paused, lost in thoughts of his old friend.

'Go on.' Mary roused him from his day-dream.

'I'm getting a transfer to East India House. Mr Pierson has promised to be one of my guarantors and so has brother John. They have to vouch for my good behaviour and forfeit a sum of money if I play the goat!' His smile was whimsical.

'Is it another clerkship?'

'Yes. Prospects are better there than at South Sea House. I – I suppose I'm very lucky.'

Mary turned her penetrating gaze on him. 'Lucky? I think you should have said *plucky*, my dear Charley.'

Her brother squeezed her hand affectionately.

'No. I'm very ordinary, Mary. Don't put me on a pedestal, I might find it difficult to keep my balance!'

Within the next few days Charles went to Blakesware

again to tell his grandmother of the recent happenings in the Temple. He was half ashamed to admit, even to himself, that he was longing to see Anne again – Anne of the fair hair and laughing blue eyes.

Mrs Field embraced him with an unusual show of affection and he was surprised to see tears on her sunken cheeks.

'My dear boy! You look tired! Now sit down and tell me your news. How is everyone?'

Briefly Charles told her of Mr Salt's death as she rocked silently to and fro in her favourite chair in the chimney corner.

'That means you're the man of the house now, Charley,' the old lady said as he finished. 'Your father's gone to pieces, as I always said he would, and poor Mary's moithered brains won't stand too much strain, you know.' She looked at him shrewdly. This undersized, delicate youth, for all his quiet, gentle ways, was showing a stronger character and a finer sense of responsibility than she had ever dreamed he possessed.

Charles paced restlessly up and down the flagged kitchen.

'I promise I won't fail them, Grandmother.' He paused and looked out of the window where the green lanes beckoned. 'I think I'll take a walk. I feel the need of fresh air.'

With an ironic smile Mrs Field watched him go. When he returned an hour or two later she saw the sparkle of excitement in his eyes.

'Well? Did you meet her, my boy?' the old lady asked quietly.

Charles faced her, astonished at her perception.

'Do you *know*, Grandmother? Do you know – Anne?'

'Did you think I didn't?' she countered with a wry smile.

'Then you know what a wonderful girl she is!' the youth sighed ecstatically. 'My lovely fair haired maid – !' A sonnet was forming in his mind.

'Come, come, my boy!' his grandmother interrupted him briskly, 'that sort of nonsense won't *do*!'

Charles looked out to the garden as he asked tensely, 'Why won't it do? Am I to be denied everything?'

'You must deny yourself love,' old Mrs Field said decisively. 'There's insanity in the Lamb family. You must not encourage this girl.'

Charles turned a shade paler and his hands clenched by his side. He kept silent with an effort, afraid of saying anything to hurt his grandmother. With sudden intuition he knew that she was nearing the end of her life.

He took her worn old hands in his with a tender gesture and his eyes were sad.

'I'll remember that, Grandmother.'

It was the last time he saw her, for she died not long after this visit, at a ripe old age. But Anne remained in Charles' mind for many years, a beautiful, tantalising shadow, the 'golden girl' of his dreams.

The seventeen-year-old lad took up his new appointment at East India House on 5th April, 1792, and went at once into the Accountant's Department.

The East India Company was a vast trading concern with offices in Leadenhall Street. Indigo and tea, drugs and piece-goods poured in a continual stream into its warehouses and were sold periodically at the auctions held in the great sale-room of the India House.

The accounts of this diverse business passed through the department of which Charles was a member.

'I have no head for figures,' he told Mary, 'I cannot think why they trust me with their books!'

'They *trust* you,' she replied fondly, 'but it's a pity the books are only ledgers. Now, tell me about your new place, Charley. Is it very big?'

He sat at the table, opposite her, in their favourite places.

'It's very big, as City offices go, and it deals in all sorts of exotic goods. But I would as soon write about the places than put down the cost of the goods they produce!'

'Yes – East India sounds romantic!' Mary smoothed her plain grey stuff dress and adjusted her mob cap more firmly on her head. 'What is your office like? Is it comfortable?'

'Comfortable?' her brother laughed. 'It might be if I were a horseman, but as I've never worn boots or mounted a horse in my life, I can't say. Why, even the room's compartments are called compounds, and each one holds six quill-driving clerks! Do you know what I call them? A collection of simples!'

Mary laughed. When Charles was in a humorous mood she enjoyed every moment of it.

'Simples! That's a new noun for clerks!'

'And a descriptive one, believe me! Our seats are so absurdly high that to get down from them is worse than getting down from a horse. They ought to provide us with stirrups!'

'Then you might get the bit between your teeth and run away!'

'Not a hope! We're railed in – separated from the mere laity by a railing that's even higher than our desks. Anyone approaching us – the lords of commerce – has to keep his distance and look up to us! Sometimes I feel like a judge looking down at his court-room. Other times I feel like a prisoner in the dock – '

Charles' lighthearted description of the accountant's office was a true one. The clerks were a happy bunch of fellows on the whole who soon discovered that the newcomer was a friendly, likeable chap, once his natural reserve had been broken down.

Some of them, like John Chambers, the Vicar of Redway's son, rode to the office on horseback and gently chaffed Charles about his regular morning and evening walk at such a sedate pace through the City streets.

'I couldn't browse at the bookstalls from the back of a horse!' Charles retorted good-humouredly.

'Now, confess, you love the London streets,' Dodwell teased, 'I've often seen you beaming at the very cobbles and the mud.'

'Why, of course I love London – every inch of it! It's *my* city, my birthplace. I like the crowds, the print shops, the coffee houses with the steam of appetising soups coming up from the kitchen – oh, and a hundred other things besides.'

'I'd as soon walk in a quiet country lane, with the hills and the sky for company,' Plumley, a youth fresh from a country village, spoke nostalgically and caressed the heads of the two hounds he had leashed under his desk.

'Too lonely!' Charles pronounced. 'Give me the Strand, or Fleet Street, where it's impossible to be dull. The lighted shops, the people themselves, have a friendly glow about them that you won't find elsewhere. Even the bustle round Covent Garden is fascinating.'

'But wicked,' said John Chambers in mock reproof, 'fie upon you, Charley.'

'It's *life*!' said Charles. 'London is like a pantomime,

full of colour and gaiety yet touched with pathos – !'

'My! The fellow's a poet!' Brook Pulham, a clerk with a gift for portraiture joined the group preparing to go to their usual chop-house punctually at one o'clock. 'I'll tell you what, Charley – I'd like to draw you sometime when you're holding forth like that! You'd make a marvellous sketch!'

Charles laughed and reached for his hat. 'Any portrait of me must look suitably grave and businesslike, so that the governors of the East India Company may cherish it for posterity!'

Laughing and joking the young men made their way to their favourite haunt, where a substantial meal kept them going until they left their desks at four in the afternoon.

There was no doubt about Charles' growing popularity, although he was neither a neat nor accurate accountant. He made frequent mistakes which he was in the habit of wiping out with his little finger, but Mr Ogilvie, the chief clerk, knew that he was conscientious and utterly reliable, and somehow his work passed muster.

Charles was quick to take advantage of the clerks' privilege of free postage and scribbled most of his private letters in his spare moments. Sometimes he used the loose leaves of his ledger to jot down chance thoughts as they came to him, and quite often these thoughts were of Anne and her fair beauty.

Life was settling into a routine when the Lamb family were again disturbed. They had to leave the Temple – they could no longer occupy the rooms that had been Mr Salt's.

'Where shall we go, Charley?' John Lamb looked helplessly at his younger son.

Charles looked round the dear familiar room which

held all his childhood memories. One by one he saw the members of his family – ageing, infirm and tormented – looking to him for guidance.

'Don't worry,' he said quietly, controlling his stammer with difficulty, 'I'll find new lodgings for us all.'

At seventeen, Charles Lamb was older than his years, yet he felt the burden of responsibility descend on him with almost painful physical impact.

His duty lay along the hard path of sacrifice. He must earn a regular salary to help his family. In his heart he knew the final struggle was over and he resigned himself to the drudgery of the desk.

Epilogue

For the rest of his working life – thirty-three years in all – Charles Lamb remained a clerk at East India House.

He was barely twenty-one when he had an attack of madness, but this did not last long and was the only one he had.

Tragedy overtook the family when Mary, in a fit of frenzy, killed her mother and injured her father. Mr Lamb and Aunt Hetty did not live long after this and Charles was left to share his solitude with a sister who had regular attacks of insanity throughout her life. He was only twenty-two when he assumed complete responsibility for Mary but he was the equal of any man in principle and courage.

As he grew older he became more independent and free thinking, but his judgment was always shrewd and humorous, his talk balanced between fun and seriousness, puns and wisdom; a passionate friend of truth in all things. The impediment in his speech never left him and for this reason he was shy of strangers and sometimes misunderstood by them.

In spite of sorrow his destiny was to write and he wrote poems, sonnets, blank verse, some plays, and under the pen-name 'Elia' (borrowed from his friend in South Sea House) wrote some of the most exquisite and expressive prose of his age.

He often collaborated with Mary and some of the best known of their joint works are the *Tales from Shakespeare* and *Mrs Leicester's School*, but there are many others specially written for the young.

Charles Lamb was also one of the greatest letter writers of his day. His correspondence with his friends, among whom were some of the greatest literary geniuses of that time, is most interesting to read.

An attack of erysipelas after a slight fall proved fatal and Lamb died on 27th December, 1834, at the age of fifty-nine, five months after his lifelong friend, Coleridge. He was buried in Edmonton Churchyard and when Mary died thirteen years later she too was buried there.

Many books have been written about Charles Lamb but the best known are those by Thomas Noon Talfourd, his intimate friend for twenty years, and *The Life of Charles Lamb* by E. V. Lucas.

But the best way to get to know a writer well is to read his works. Lamb's poems and essays reveal his gentle, sensitive character as no biographer can, and paint a vivid picture of the age in which he lived.